Volume One

His
Chosen Bride

*Living Out Your Position
as Daughter of the King,
and Bride of Christ...*

Jennifer J. Lamp

GraceWorks Ministry Press
Wichita, KS

Preliminary Edition

Although this book is protected under the copy right laws of the United States, and thus the copying for commercial gain or profit is prohibited, the copying of an occasional page for group study or encouragement of others is welcomed.

Dedication:

This book is dedicated to

Melissa Joy Perry,

who has now become
Mrs. Rob Robbins,
for the ways in which God used her
to plant within my heart
the desire to aim for that which is
higher, purer and sweeter.

For the selfless way in
which she allowed me to observe
God's working in her life,
and the investments that she made
in mine as she lived singly,
and beautifully unto the Lord.

And of course to my parents,
who have loved me endlessly,
prayed for me tirelessly,
and challenged me unceasingly
in the ways of God's Word.
No child has been so blessed as I.

Forward

Belonging to Jesus
Sold out to Him.
Saying "Yes" to His plans
and His voice...realizing
that being His bride is
the ultimate of all callings...

This is the beautiful,
vibrant message
in Jennifer's new book
to single women.
She calls these women
to the heart of God
where He can then use them
in a broken world,
with hurting people.

(continued)

Can you be content, for now,
as the bride of Christ?
Can you set aside a period
of time... and all your
longings and desires...
to serve Him exclusively?
Can you trust Him with
your future? With a mate?
With His timing and plan
for your life?

In a humble, quiet way, Jennifer,
using what she has personally
learned, tells stories that
are powerful and true.
Read these pages.
Open your hesitant, fearful
heart. Be joyful where you
are, and let God do miracles
through you. The sunrises
will come, in time, if we
are faithful with today.

Ann Kiemel Anderson
Clovis, California

Preface

When the Lord asked Moses to stand before Pharaoh, he immediately felt inadequate and asked "Why me, Lord? Don't you know I stutter and am not equaled to this task?" Yet when God calls, he is not looking for talent or gifted-ness, but a person through whom He can show His strength, which is often more noticed in one who knows they are especially small in themselves. God told Moses "Now therefore go, and I will be with thy mouth, and teach thee what thou shalt say." (Ex. 4:12) When the Lord laid it on my heart to begin this book, I felt very much like I imagine Moses did. It quite frankly frightened me to think of writing such a book, yet compared to Moses' task of speaking those strong words to an ungodly king, my job seems to hold somewhat less fear and trepidation. Yet there is an element of that as well, as I seek to correctly share what He has laid on my heart in the way that would be pleasing to Him.

I have thought often of Jesus when He stated that He spoke not His own words, but the words of the Father. Though that seems an overwhelming thought, it is my prayer that my words here would reflect not my own heart, but that of my Father's, and that by reading these words not only would you desire to follow Him more radiantly, but most importantly, that you would come to love him more deeply.

As I look at others, those that God has used to so greatly impact my life, I realize that there are many who are more worthy to write such a book, yet the Lord has clearly laid it upon my heart to write it. Possibly I will find His primary purpose in involving me in this work is that I will have the opportunity to read and study His Word more carefully myself, for the shortcomings of my own life are ever in need of "more of Him."

The greater part of this book is simply the organizing of thoughts and principles of His Word that have been gleaned from others throughout the years. Were all the "authors" of this book listed, and their influences on my life described, another volume would need to be added to contain. It is with much gratefulness to God and to them that this book has been brought about and is in your hands even now.

The rest of the book is sharing from my own struggles my own selfishness, and the unrelenting faithfulness of the Lord to continue to lovingly, patiently seek to mold each of us into His likeness.

After working on this for quite some time, I ask a friend, who has published many books, how one knows that a book is actually finished. He said "Your time runs out so you say a prayer and a hearty 'Amen!'" So as I say my "Amen!", my promise to you is that, though imperfect, I will do my best to share with you, as a friend in the pages of this book, the exciting wonderful, yet sometimes painful, ways God has worked in my own life, as well in as the lives of those around me whom I look up to and dearly love. May God's blessing be upon this work, not because of any of my words, but because of the living message that He, our beloved Bridegroom, desires to portray in each of our lives as His chosen bride.

Jennifer Lamp
November 18, '99

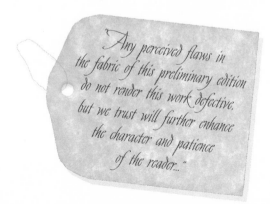

"Any perceived flaws in the fabric of this preliminary edition do not render this work defective, but we trust will further enhance the character and patience of the reader..."

The Story Behind this Book...

My mother often shared with women's Bible study groups that she taught that the picture of the Proverbs 31 woman was not a story of this woman's day, but of her life. The focus is that whatever she was doing she was giving it her best and offering it to the Lord. It has also been said that when approaching the Word of God, there is one interpretation (God's divine, original intention), yet many applications.

I don't know about you, dear reader, but whenever I used to think about "the Proverbs 31 woman" I always pictured her in her only in her wifely role. I certainly recognized the benefit of emulating the things she did and the person she was, but I saw it as a picture of who I wanted to be as a wife. Certainly I saw the importance of speaking in kindness, with wisdom, being a diligent worker, and knew that I could begin now to develop in these areas. At the same time, I considered that most of the traits were those which should be learned in preparation for marriage, should the Lord bring that about. This was a paradigm that was about to be changed...

Years ago I was encouraged to begin the habit of reading a Proverb each day. On the first day of the month I would read Proverbs 1, and so on. Since most months do not have 31 days, I looked forward to those months with the extra day. Last October, Halloween, happened of course to be one such day. Although I often have dreaded this day, it is certainly a that the Lord created, the eve of Reformation Day, a day where Christ already has the victory. On this particular evening I thought of the verse in Romans 12 ("Do not be overcome with evil, overcome evil with good") and decided to spend my evening alone with the Lord.

As I read the passage from Proverbs 31, the prayer of my heart was that He would show me how to lift up His name that night in a way that would glorify Him. I prayed that somehow, in my little corner, good would overcome evil on that twisted evening. With that thought in mind, I read through this chapter perhaps more pensively than before. For some reason for the first time I saw verse 10, "A wife of noble character who can find..." in light of Isaiah 54 which states,

"Thy Maker is thine husband...." I had always hoped and prayed that I would be that wife of noble character if God ever called me to that place, but it had never occurred to me that I could be that wife even now, serving Him as my husband. I suddenly became excited as I read each verse, seeing the analogies that could be made for us as single women and thus the Lord laid it upon my heart to begin this book.

Now, several months and hundreds of hours later, the Lord is bringing it to completion as it seems we are just days away from going to press. The chapters that follow are not earth-shattering, but rather contain heartfelt thoughts about some of the ways that God uses to mold and shape our lives that we might be more pleasing to Him. As this journey continues, His hand being steadfast to teach and to guide, I am confident I will desire to add new chapters, just as I am sure the roads God has taken *you* down could add profitable chapters to a book such as this. Yet, apart from the Word of God Itself, no book penned by human hands could ever be complete, for we "see through a glass darkly." But what comfort can be taken from Scripture *"when we see Him, we shall be like Him, for we shall see Him as He is."*

Truly, He is the one that has brought it together and continued to lovingly train me in the process. I cannot count the times that I have just "happened" to hear even just one sentence in passing that has provided vital insight and balance for the book. In some ways I fear handing it over, as I know that in the very next week there will be countless changes that "should have been made." Yet in the midst of it all, if the Lord would chose to use even the very weaknesses of this child to reveal more clearly and brightly the strength of Himself, then may it be to His glory.

A Few Helpful Notes:

• At the end of each chapter I will include a section full of helpful verses, books and tools that pertain to what we have discussed. If this is an area in which you would like more guidance or support, these might be helpful to you. Many of these will be Scriptures and you will find that as you memorize them and then meditate on them, God will do His work in your heart through the power of His Word. If you would desire to obtain any of the materials that are mentioned, feel free to contact us at the address in back, and we will either make it available to you ourselves, or let you know how you might find it elsewhere.

• Perhaps I should mention that years ago my sister and I were privileged to start "GraceWorks," a planning & ministry organizer for use by moms and single women. Many of the experiences that I share have been a part of my involvement with this, and so you will likely hear me refer to the "planners" or "GraceWorks" from time to time. Additionally, as I have written, it has seemed logical to occasionally note specific *pages* that seem to be helpful in supporting the goals of various chapters.

• I have chosen to make some grammatical alterations, even at the risk of being improper. We have chosen to capitalize pronouns used in Scripture which are referring to any part of the Trinity, even if the original text does not. Likewise, we have purposely not capitalized the name of the evil one, even though this may go against standard grammatical rules.

• Finally, many of the pronouns that are used in this book, have been placed into the female gender (she, her, etc.), simply because I am not writing to men. Were my audience more general in nature, I would have used male pronouns for general usage.

Acknowledgements

I would like to express my deepest gratefulness to my dear parents & precious sister for their encouragement throughout the years, what wonderful and hilarious memories we have shared. I must specifically thank them for their eleventh hour assistance in bringing this book to print (and eleventh hour assistance with every other project I've undertaken!). Mom was my chief advisor through it all, and Dad helped me fashion one of his famous "to do lists," on one of his legal pads (complete with markers, boxes and symbols)~ as only he could, to move me toward completion. Wendy gave timely counsel & kept me from getting too serious in it all~ her laughter came at all the right times. I love you all so dearly.

A thank you goes out to BBN radio for the insightful Biblical teaching that they faithfully broadcast across the country and world, and the blessing that continual feeding has been to me.

Also to the Institute in Basic Life Principles ministry which has challenged our family to seek God's principles in every area of life, contributing greatly to many of the thoughts laid out in this book.

I am grateful to Ann Kiemel Anderson for her encouragement and challenge to make this book better.

I cannot thank my Aunt Ann Lamp and Eldora Brock enough for the hours they invested in editing a very challenging manuscript. Among other things, a one hundred and seventy-eight-word run-on sentence was discovered... Truly they had their work cut out for them but never flinched or faltered. To them, to Dr. Woychuk, to the Monday night Bible Study group, and others that happened to be still a moment too long and were handed a chapter, I give my thanks.

Speaking for my Aunt Ann and Eldora, I would like to thank those responsible for adjusting the rules of English grammar, allowing prepositions to now be placed at the end of a sentence (where I have always felt they really belonged), making the editing much of this book much simpler. Now, if it could just be decided that it is acceptable to say "he that" instead of "he who," their future editing jobs would be aided immensely.

Special thanks also goes to Candy Wilson for her diligent efforts in "running" GraceWorks as I wrote, and to Natalie Wickham for last minute editing.

Above all, I thank my Lord Jesus for loving and saving one that was most unlovable, and for entrusting to her a task that was far beyond her own ability to accomplish...

To Him be the Glory!

Table of Contents

A Favorite!

"And they received the Word of God

with all readiness of mind, and searched the Scriptures daily,

whether those things were so" Acts 17:11

This gives two wonderful principles to live by.
First of all, the Bereans received teaching "with readiness
of mind". They were not leaning far back in their chairs,
maintaining skeptical expressions, they were leaning forward and eager to learn! At the same time, they were
diligent in knowing God's Word. When they were
taught, they would return to the Scriptures to confirm that
what they were learning was indeed truth. It is the perfect balance between being enthusiastic learners yet being
careful that we are only believing what God has said to
be truth. I love this balance and hope that you too will
claim it as your own as you read this book, and
with all other teaching you receive!

Who can find a Virtuous Woman?

For Her Price is Far Above Rubies.

My new *Friend…* How excited I am for the opportunity to write to you in this way. For I do not feel that I am truly writing a book, but rather a very long letter to someone I dearly love. And this is not just any letter, it is one written from my heart to yours, sharing a vision that has been given to me from a hundred different directions and experiences. Some of them bring back the most beautiful recollections, others bring memories of tears, but when all mixed together they become the factors that God has used to lovingly teach me more of His ways and show me that I am ever needing more of Him.

I realize as I write, that all of you are at different stages in your walk of life and in your relationship with the Lord. Some of you have known Him for as long as you can remember and have opened this book with the desire to deepen and broaden that walk even further. Others of you are just beginning to experience some of the wonder and excitement of living your life for Christ and are seeking to be more effective for Him today than you thought possible yesterday. Some of you are eager to follow the Lord, but are uncertain of how that can be accomplished in our day and age. Certainly, others of you are discouraged because you have been a Christian for many years, but still feel like the fruit of it shows little in your life. The struggle with sin and self seems too great at times to overcome. And finally, I'm sure that some of you have been given this book by one who loves you, but if you were to be honest, you would rather throw it across the room than be reading it now. For those of you, I would like to ask you a simple question: "Are you happy in life now?" And if the answer is no, then you have nothing to lose in reading this "letter." I hope that you will stay with it and I would love to hear from you as you finish.

For all of you I pray that this book offers you a vision that will inspire you from the bottom of your heart. Satan has tried to cause us to think that we are insignificant during this time in our lives, that we cannot really do anything effective for the Lord until we arrive at a "real" life, being an adult, being married, having children, etc. Until then we tend to think that this is kind of our own time, and we can easily lose sight of the exciting opportunities that we have right in front of us. This should come as no surprise as it is during this very time that we can do some of the greatest damage to satan's dark kingdom! Nothing would delight him more than for us to spend it frivolously for that which does not count.

I hope to come alongside, challenging you toward something higher, toward setting aside what is typical that you might make a radical difference in your world for Christ. Have you ever realized the opportunity you have before you? We will be talking about many individuals that have chosen to rise above, to make a difference. What about you? Do you have a vision for where to get started?

In I Corinthians 2:15 it describes us as a sweet-smelling aroma to God and to those who are saved ("For we are to God the fragrance of Christ...") The other paints us as shining like stars in the universe (Phil. 2:15) Wow! What inspiring thoughts! When people think of you, of your life, when you enter a room ~ would either of these pictures come to their minds? Do you refresh those around you with the sweetness of "Christ in you, the hope of glory?" Do you shine and radiate for Him in such a way that others are drawn to desire more of Him themselves? Well, that is what this book is about. How we might shine brightly for Him and make a difference in a world that is very dark and without hope.

If you are like me, all of these things sound good, but yet a little beyond reach. Does one simply get up one morning and decide that she is going to be a light for Christ and seek to make an impact on those that God places around her? Well yes... and no. It certainly must be a decision that we make each day, yet just as most jobs require skill and training, so do we as we shine for Him. God's Word must always remain our chief "teacher," for no matter how many wonderful books and instructors there are, our Lord Jesus is the only One with the true answers. He is the One who knows all we need in life, and lovingly teaches us how to experience His joy even in trials, and not only that, He also supplies the power to meet the struggles therein! If you have not already spent time with Him today, set this book aside and pick up His Book and begin to read. Ask Him to give you a "hunger and thirst for righteousness," for more of Him if you feel a lack of desire right now. I have prayed this prayer before, and He has abundantly answered. He is our Chief Teacher, the One in Whom we ultimately must find all of our answers.

Yet what a gift He has given us in each other. What a blessing it is to look at the lives of others who have gone before us in the faith and to learn from their lives and experiences. What a blessing to read of the lives of Joseph, of David, of Ruth, of Esther, of Paul. To see the triumphs that God brought to their lives, the victories, and even the forgiveness and restoration after sin. God was good to give these glimpses of His influence upon our flesh, our humanity, that we might see the power He wants to display in our own lives. We have also been blessed to have biographies of those who have lived in more recent times who have stood for Him, even in the face of death and persecution. Few of us have been required to go through the horrors that many have experienced, yet what beautiful "vessels of honor" the Lord has made of these individuals, often even because of these very experiences. And finally, we have those who are living testimonies around us today, possibly our own parents, people in our church, pastors, speakers, or authors whose words we have read. God *allows us to watch these men and women of the faith and as we see the way that He has worked in their lives, we gain a deeper understanding of what He desires to do in our own. And we must know that He can work these things in us~ for He loves us all the same. The same grace He gives to another He also gives to you!*

Once we begin growing in His grace, we begin to see the desperate needs of others around. We should begin to be aware of the urgency to fulfill the Great Commission, that we might be used of God to warn many of the perilous road that they are traveling. To share with them the antidote they desperately need to rescue them from the judgement of a Holy God.

Though we need to have a burning in our hearts to share His truth, there is something more. We must also live in such a way that people desire what we have. If we try to share Christ but do not have His character and radiance about our lives, we are in danger of damaging the very goal for which we are striving. But if people see a true difference in our lives, if we are bright shining lights for Him, if we are continually seeking to have a pure love for others, then a great door to share what He has done in our lives is opened.

So then, this book is a combination of what God would have us to be on the inside, but also on the outside, our manners, our conversation, our actions. It is all a single package, one that needs to be worked on as a whole. For as God changes our hearts, it will affect our whole being~ what we think, the things that we say, even the daily decisions that we make. And we do this both to please the Lord and with the desire that nothing that is seen or heard outwardly would detract from what God is doing on the inside.

Do you desire a life that is radically different, one that is sold out to Him, to be a beautiful treasure for Him to look down upon? Well then, I am glad you're here. For although no book other than the Bible could give us a complete picture of what we can be for Him, what you hold in your hands is an attempt to pass along a piece of this vision to you, with the prayerful hope that you will also become excited about giving the time you have right now to Him in a dynamic way that you will never regret.

We will talk in a later chapter about our opportunity as women to be the "heart "of our community, the heart of our families, the heart of the body of Christ. Think of this as you read, and begin to consider some of the implications it might have in your own life as you seek to be His heart to the world around.

The first few chapters give background that might help you to know more about me and the philosophy of the book. Then, together we will look at many different areas that we daily confront in life and talk about how our Savior wants to be "Lord" of these areas. But please don't skip these first few chapters, for I don't want this book to stop with you. As you begin to catch this vision for yourself, I hope that you will become contagious and pass it on to others. And not just what I have said, but what God has been teaching you along the way. As we are doing this we must always remember that far more important than looking like we have it together on the outside, is what is truly in our hearts for Him. As I Corinthians 13 exhorts, we can do many wonderful things, but if we do it without love in our hearts for God and others, it is all as nothing. As nothing! So while the latter chapters often focus on what we can do outwardly to radiate Christ, the first chapters are a vital background for the chapters to come. All in all, I pray that as your understanding and excitement for things of the Lord deepens, that you will combine it with the lessons that God has taught you thus far that you might create a "vision" of your own that you could pass on to others with the same zeal in which I am writing to you now.

Speaking of others, I would highly recommend that you would choose a friend or mentor (even a mother or grandmother!) who would go through this book along with you. If it is a friend who is close in age, possibly you will be able to strengthen one another in spirit as you discuss the challenges this book contains. If your friend is younger, what a wonderful opportunity you will have to encourage her in the ways of God. And if you work through this with a mentor, I am certain that her own experiences and insight will only enrich what the Lord is working in your own heart along the way. There are questions at the end of each chapter to help you lift the principles out of the book and into your own daily life. The more you invest yourself as you read and answer the questions, the more benefit you will receive and dynamic changes you will experience, as the Lord works in your life and heart.

Whatever your age may be, the simple fact that you are single gives you an incredible opportunity to become all you can for Him at this time in your life. For though you might be busy doing many different things, there may never be such an opportunity again to make your life "rich in Him" as you have right now. As you seek to know and love Him as a single person, not only will your ability to bless those around you increase and deepen, but your ability to bless and be an incredible helpmeet *mate* to a man that God would bring into your life as husband will multiply many times over as well. Whatever God has for your future, you will have no regrets for using these single years of your life to His glory, nor regrets having missed out on the many wonderful, purposeful opportunities that are so plentiful during these years!

At the end of each chapter I will ask a series of questions. These are to help you consider what you have just read in light of your own life. Many of the questions even challenge you to consider a plan of action. Though we would love to be able to read a book and put the things right into action, we certainly know that most often this is a process. You might be helped by keeping a notebook with you to give you more room as you answer the questions, and for additional thoughts you may have. Be encouraged to know that in the last chapter of the book, a plan is given to go back and begin implementing each of these chapters into your life! Best of all, the Holy Spirit promises to "guide us unto all truth," and ultimately He is our teacher (and reminder) as we walk through life.

My first challenge to you is that as you read this book, that you will ask the Lord to come in and do His mighty work in every area of your life. My words will be worth little if they lack the empowerment of the Holy Spirit. Ask that you would have a consuming desire for more of Him as you read His Word and spend time with Him each day. And may this book take you by the hand and lead you through some of these areas as you walk this road with Him...

The heart of her Husband

doth

safely

trust in

her...

A diamond is bestowed as a symbol of love. It is the dream of every young girl~ a beautiful ring... and the adoring suitor behind it! Yet did you know that God has already sought you as His Bride? Read in Isaiah 54 as the Lord calls Himself our husband!

> *"Sing, O barren woman, you who never bore a child; burst into song, shout for joy, you who were never in labor; because more are the children of the desolate woman than of her who has a husband. Enlarge the place of your tent... do not hold back.. strengthen your stakes...*
>
> *For your Maker is your Husband–*
> *the LORD Almighty is His name– the Holy One of Israel is your Redeemer... the God of all the earth..."*

Truly, as He has claimed you, you are already complete in Him! The Proverbs 31 woman was compared to a ruby. We might at first wonder why this was not a diamond until we realize that a ruby is even more rare and more valuable than a diamond! God gave you the most valuable engagement ring ever given, comprised of a drop of His Son's precious blood~ the ruby. You are loved and cherished by Him!

The Power of Love

Lenin once said, "Give me a handful of dedicated men, and I will control the world." It is frightening to see what those "few" men were able to do and their continuing effects upon our world today. Yet the principle is true. Determination and dedication can often take one where talent and riches cannot. But what is the secret of being fully dedicated? Is it not love–loving the thing to which we are dedicated? Let's consider for a moment the men that followed Lenin. Although they may not have loved him, their passionate belief in his causes, and their desire for power, aroused in them a selfish love of his ideals. If these men were able to accomplish so much, to have such a damaging effect upon so vast a number of people because of their admiration and passion, how much more might we be able to bless and do good as a result of our love for God and His ways? If this be so, then if we desire to succeed in our quest to please God and edify others, we must allow Him to cultivate in our hearts a deep, abiding love for Him.

Do you really love God? Do I? I have been challenged during the last few years to deepen my understanding of what it really means to love God. I had always thought I loved God, and would have responded enthusiastically if I would have been questioned on this point. Yet after I heard the teaching of a pastor on this subject, I realized that I too closely equated obeying, serving, worshipping and fearing God with loving Him. Certainly these are all noble acts, but it is frightful to consider that it is possible to do all of these things without love in our hearts for Him. And although they should come in response to this love (and certainly are evidence of that love~ Jn 14:21), it never occurred to me that one could do all of those things without loving God, nor that loving God was in some way a separate issue. In my mind, to love God more meant to be more obedient, to spend more time in prayer, to be more faithful. But He desired that I simply focus on Him and as He deepened my love, I could trust Him to produce these beautiful responses in my heart.

Directing our Thoughts

"Love the Lord... with all thy heart... soul... mind... strength..." Mk 12:30

A when a girl becomes engaged, it is nearly impossible to keep her from talking about the one she loves. Of course, she does not say things like "He is 6'3, has jet black hair, and five members in his family..." Rather, she would say: "Oh, he is so wonderful, he is so incredible. It was so dear when he said this or did that. Oh, how I love him!" She becomes "filled up" with his wonder. Time spent with him, the giving spirit toward him, the praising of his finer qualities~ are not done out of obligation or because she feels she *has to*, but she has grown in fondness and affection toward him. Though he might possess some truly honorable qualities, she is still making a choice, choosing to place her affections on him.

Have you ever done that with the Lord? Have you ever curled up in a chair and done nothing but "set your affections on Him?" Have you quietly meditated on His goodness, His mercy, His love? Don't allow your love for Him to exist within you unenjoyed! He is after all, our "husband!" and loving Him should bring joy to our hearts!

An Unexpected Result

Most amazingly, the more I focused on loving Him, the more I felt loved *of* Him. We have an example of this transfer of affection~ from following Him as Lord, to loving Him as Savior in Hosea 2:16 *"...in that day," Says the Lord, "That you will call Me 'My Husband,' And no longer call me 'My Master.'"* (NKJV) After I began to focus on loving Him, prayer was such a natural desire. I did not feel I had to struggle to be heard~ I knew He was right there~ I felt as if His arms were tight around me.

Of course, He loved me no more than before, I just began to realize His love in a brand new way. Certainly years before, in response to that love, I had come to love Him too, but realized only a small part of the joy He intended me to experience in that love. It was like an endless supply of sugar cubes in my pocket which were there all along, but whose sweetness was yet to be tasted.

The Treasure He's Given

One element that dramatically separates Christianity from the religions of the world is our foundational belief in a personal God who loves us. Our God is not distant. He wants to be an active part of your life. Of mine. In fact, He wrote us a letter telling us of His love and care for us. Just as we would be eager to read a letter from one we love, we should have a passion to daily read and learn from the Word of God, recollecting upon the great treasure therein. Let's take a moment to glimpse into the heart of King David as he considers the incomparable worth of the Scriptures in Psalm 19:

> *"The law of the LORD is perfect, converting the soul;*
> *The testimony of the LORD is sure, making wise the simple;*
> *The statutes of the LORD are right, rejoicing the heart;*
> *The commandment of the LORD is pure, enlightening the eyes;*
> *The fear of the LORD is clean, enduring forever;*
> *The judgments of the LORD are true and righteous altogether.*
> *More to be desired are they than gold, Yea, than much fine gold...*

More to Consider

As our love for Him deepens, we must be careful that we do not become flippant or casual about His majesty, His holiness. Our hearts should never cease from attributing to Him the uncomprehendible nature of Himself, the One around whom the six-winged creatures fly, resting not day or night proclaiming "Holy, holy holy..."

How do we guard against becoming too casual in this area? Certainly a study of Revelation reminds us of the startling honor due His Name. Often we err because we only consider certain aspects of God. By looking only upon His love or grace, we build a distorted picture in our minds of who He is. Yes He is gracious, yes He is loving! But He is also a "dreadful" God (Daniel 9:4), a God that will one day judge the wicked, asking them to account for what they have done.

We also must have a holy fear of God. Perhaps the best way to define this right now would be by saying that although God loves us, He is still holy and pure in a way that we cannot imagine. That purity caused Him to turn His face when His own beloved Son hung nailed to a tree with the weight of our sins upon Him. Realizing that God sees us all the time and knows what we do in secret, and every thought that courses through our minds. This can be both a great comfort or frightful thought, depending on our relationship and degree of obedience to Him. God is always lovingly watching and is the *"rewarder of those that diligently seek Him."* He also knows that we will never be happy following our own ways and as a father lovingly disciplines his children, so He disciplines us, with our very best in mind.

Beyond our Emotions

And finally, we can never be dependent on our emotions to direct our behavior. There will be times that we don't feel like doing what is right, just as there are times a child does not feel like going to bed when his parents know he must. There will be days that we will need to stand against our very selves in order to follow His ways~ just as He taught us in the garden of Gethsemane, when he denied His Own will for the will of the Father. It is an opportunity for us to express our commitment and resolve to follow Him. And as our love for God and His ways increase, the more joyous our service will become. Perhaps you have heard the story about the little boy struggling to carry his little brother. Someone said to him "My, it looks like he is heavy!" To which the little boy responded "he's not heavy, he's my brother!" Love makes easy what mere obligation calls a chore.

Have You "Fallen In Love?"

Are you resting, content in loving Him today? Not just in serving Him, or in fearing Him, not even just in obeying Him, but in *loving Him.* For if we focus on the greater, the lesser areas will follow as a natural result, as they are indeed fruits of a right relationship. It was with this thought that I wanted to begin, because though I will be sharing many ways in which we might *live out* the message of Him in our hearts and lives in practical ways, we must never forget the issue of highest importance, that we never lose sight of *loving* the Lord as Mark 12:30 exhorts~for this is the greatest commandment and the one from which everything else must stem. The title of this chapter reflects the trust that that the husband of our Proverbs 31 woman had in her. (To make our reading easier in this book, we will refer henceforth to this revered unnamed woman as "Yaqar," a Hebrew word meaning *"rare, to make precious, to be prized").* Does God, as your heavenly husband, have reason to trust you to be faithful to Him? If you are struggling, ask Him to deepen your love for Him. As your love for Him deepens, so the joy in your dedication to Him will be multiplied.

Have You Taken the First Step?

I could never assume that each person reading this book has a personal relationship with the Lord Jesus. The only reason we are able to love Him, is because He first loved us. When a man and women love each other, they make the commitment of marriage, saying vows, proclaiming they will remain together "for better or worse, in sickness and in health." God created this very special relationship to be a visible example of His love and commitment to us. And just as both individuals must agree to marriage, so we must "receive" the proposal that has been offered us by our Bridegroom, the Lord Jesus. His marriage commitment is not for this life only, but for all eternity!

In order to have an accurate picture of our true need of Him, we must realize that we have sinned against Him in the most awful way. We may compare ourselves with others and think that we are nearly perfect, yet compared to the bright righteousness of Christ, we all fall far short. One lie, one hateful thought, and we have broken the law of God. As Isaiah says "each has turned to his own way." We do not even have the desire to seek after Him. Yet in the midst of our sin~ our choosing our own stubborn way, Jesus loved us and came to save us "out of a miry pit." We can refuse His offer, but if we do, then we will someday stand before God, our Judge. Though we will all stand before Him, those of us that have the "covering" of His blood over our sins will be given eternal life, and it says that our sins will forever be forgotten. But for those that enter without that covering, a great wrath awaits. Satan would have us believe that we can somehow be good enough, that we are not really so bad, and not in need of God's forgiveness. Yet if that were the case, then Jesus would have never needed to die. But we do have that need, and He did die that painful death on our behalf, in our place.

If we say to one on this earth that we will marry him, but we never make that final commitment of marriage, we of course, remain unmarried. In the same way, unless we are committed to the Lord Jesus, and clinging only to Him for salvation, we remain without a Savior.

Yet if we trust Christ to take away our sin, the Bible says that He will save us from eternal damnation *("For the wages of sin is death; but the gift of God is eternal life..." Rom. 6:23)*. If you have not asked Him to forgive your sins, and feel the Lord tugging at your heart at this moment, would you stop and pray just now? You might pray something like:

Dear Jesus, I am a sinner, worthy of punishment and separation from you. Yet You died on the cross that I might have life, that I might know you. I ask you to forgive my sins, and thank you for your promise to do just that. Infiltrate my life, and lead me in a way that is pleasing to You. Amen

If you have prayed that prayer just now, I hope that you will write me ~ I would love to send a booklet that will be helpful to you.

The Opportunity Before You!

Once we truly love Him, we will begin to reflect Him. We do not have to settle for a normal life. We have the incredible opportunity to *shine for Him.* In Philippians 2:15 God says we *"shine like lights in the world,"* another version says *"as stars in the universe."* Consider the story of Moses going upon the mountain to receive the commandments of the Lord. Remember after he descended he covered his face because of God's glory that radiated from it? I always assumed that Moses wore the covering because the glory and holiness of God would have been too much for the people to behold. But that could not have been it, for certainly Moses could not have survived such an incident either. No, they would have lived had they seen His face. Then why the covering? A radio teacher shared that in his study, he had come to the conclusion that in hiding his face, Moses was protecting the people from the holy conviction of the Lord. They were fearful because of their sin and did not want God's holy conviction stirring within their hearts.

We cannot know what the Israelites' response would have been, but it is interesting to consider what change of heart such conviction may have wrought. In their hearts it seems as if they were saying; *"Speak to us, Moses, tell us what God has said... but please Moses, don't shine... don't radiate His presence to us."* So Moses covered his face. And don't we do the same thing as Christians? We know the truth, we know what God has done for us, and we might even tell it to others if asked. *But do we shine? Do we radiate Christ in our lives?* And here lies the ultimate goal of this book, that we might consider together what it means to shine for Him and how we might encourage each other toward this goal!

Questions:

1) Have you made the ultimate commitment to Christ in entrusting your life to Him and receiving His forgiveness for your sins? Do you remember when it was or where you were?

2) What actions can you take this week to direct your heart into the love of God?

3) What are some of the characteristics and functions of light?

4) If you are light, how can you actively live out these characteristics in this world? How can you start doing this more actively right now?

Additional Support:**

• Verses: Mark 12:30, I John 4:9, Eph. 5; Eph. 3:14-21; Rom. 8:37-39
• Tools: Abiding in Christ page *(journal daily thoughts, intentions, activities)*
• Resources: *The Greatest Thing in the World... Love* (Henry Drummond) *If I thought you had this book before you now, I would tell you to set this one aside and instead read it first!*

** For lack of space, we are only listing titles and authors in this section. Most could be found using this information at your local Christian bookstore, and many we carry through GraceWorks (or can gladly provide ordering information). Feel free to call or write the address listed in the back.

...so that He shall have no need of spoil

For we are... ordained...for good works,
that we should walk in them... Eph. 2:10

$\mathcal{M}$any books have been written to instruct businesses in writing a "business plan" for their company. This is a written projection of their goals and aspirations within their entity. This allows them to maintain a clear, dynamic focus and evaluate how to wisely use time and other resources. It is a well validated fact that if a company has written goals for its future, there is a much stronger probability that the company will survive and succeed. In fact, before a business can obtain a loan from a bank, it is required to submit a business plan. The bank wants to see that they have effectively thought through their strategies, knowing having such a plan gives great increased potential for survival. What about you? Do you have a plan for your life? If someone were to ask you "What is your purpose in life?" would you have a distinct picture of it in your mind?

A Discouraging Scene

It is a sobering sight to behold most of the young people of our day. Despite their strivings to be different, they are amazingly alike in their dress and actions. They have been sold a lie, or a package of lies, really—taught to believe that they evolved from nothing and that there is no more to life than what one can get for oneself. They live for immediate gratification with little thought for the future. Often their inward insecurities are reflected outwardly by tattoos, body piercings and startling hair coloring. Others may not show such obvious markings, but their hearts are still the same, just as desperate, just as sad. Some may act as if they are truly having a great time~ and maybe in moments they are *(there is a pleasure in sin for a season)*, but follow them home when the parties are over and their friends are gone to see what little satisfaction their life really brings.

Choosing a Higher Call

God sent Amy Carmichael to rescue exploited children in India, and because of her devotion, the difference she made in their lives will never be forgotten. Her writings during that time continue to challenge and inspire many today. Do you know when she decided to follow God with all of her heart? Though it was a gradual process, there was a turning point when she turned seventeen. In Elisabeth Elliot's beautiful narrative of Amy's life, she writes:

> *"The preoccupations of seventeen-year-old girls—their looks, their clothes, their social life—do not change very much from generation to generation. But in every generation there seem to be a few who make other choices. Amy was one of the few."*

What about you? Have you chosen to be one of the few?

One Important Key

What is it that causes one person to be able to rise above the pressure of the crowd and another to be controlled by it? What causes some to seek to excel that they might make a difference in the world, to use their lives in beneficial ways, while others destroy both their own lives and others?

Certainly many factors are involved, yet one seems to stand above the others. We have all known individuals who grow up in fine families, but still get involved with the wrong people and make poor decisions, ending up devastated. At the same time, we know of those who grow up in terrible situations, yet rise above their upbringing and become quite honorable people. What is the difference? Aside from the grace of God, it seems that one of the greatest differences is a sense of purpose. Purpose makes the difference.

Though there is certainly evil purposes to be found which some young people have been caught within, most young people today are not suffering because of an evil purpose, but because of *no purpose whatsoever.* If we were to ask one who is caught up in peer pressure and lives in a world of parties and rebellion "What are you living for?" the response would likely be, "to have fun, man!" or "nothing, really" or possibly "I don't know." If I were to ask a young person who was working diligently to be a good student, was contributing to others, and using time wisely, I would not be surprised to hear in response to the same question "I want to be a doctor (or a teacher, or a counselor...)" or "I want my life to impact this world for good, to help people in some way." The first has no real purpose; the second has a valuable purpose.

"Live your life while you have it. Life is a splendid gift. There is nothing small in it, for the greatest things grow by God's law out of the smallest. But to live your life, you must discipline it. You must not fritter it away in fair purpose, erring act, inconstant will, but must make your thought, your work, your acts all work to the same end, and that end not in self but in God."

Florence Nightingale

Living Above Average

What about us as Christians? Should we not have the most valuable purpose of all, a purpose that motivates us to press on, even when we feel like giving up? It is not enough just to do *good things* from time to time. God does not want only a part of us. I heard it once taught that the significance about the widow's mite was not that he had her *mite,* but that He had *her.* I had never thought of it in quite that light before, but what a true statement of this one that gave everything she had. He wants our *whole* heart and *all* of our affections, and for those to be focused on *Him* that we might glorify Him as we follow His will. Remember His warnings about being lukewarm? He says that those *"who are not for Me are against Me"* (Matt. 12:30). That's a pretty strong statement! Certainly there is no room, and no time, for us to live average, uncommitted lives!

We also must purpose to live righteously before God. The Bible says of Daniel that *"he purposed in his heart that he would not defile himself..."* (Dan. 1:8). We are told that Ezra *"prepared his heart to seek the Law of the Lord, and to do it..."* (Ezra 7:10). Such a challenge these and others have left as they so carefully readied themselves to face struggles of life How much more should we?!

Perhaps you sang this song as a child:

> *Dare to be a Daniel, Dare to stand alone.*
> *Dare to have a purpose, and dare to make it known!*
> (Philip P. Bliss)

A Statement all Your Own!

The purpose statement is made up of the following five sections:

1) Our Ultimate Purpose: As Christians, we all begin with nearly the same statement. Matthew 22:37 says that the greatest commandment is to *"love the LORD thy God with all thy heart, and with all thy soul, and with all thy mind."* Then it continues *"the second is like unto it, Thou shalt love thy neighbor as thyself."* We might picture a purpose statement as a tree. Just as a tree must be planted in the ground, so as Christians we must be rooted in Christ. If we are not, then nothing else is of any significance, for without Him, we cannot truly live, nor can we grow and produce fruit (John 15).

2) Freedom in Truth: The trunk is the branches' support system that allows them to push toward the sun for life and to secure nourishment. We can look at the trunk as the channel that carries life-giving nutrients for the fruit-bearing parts of the tree. In our desire to produce fruit, satan would attempt to keep us from growing that fruit by stunting our growth through fear and rejection of God's Truth. Yet God has given us the weapon we need to stand strong. *"The truth shall make you free" (John 8:32).* What truths from Scripture has God used most powerfully in changing areas of weakness in your life? Have you struggled with fear, doubt, discouragement, inferiority? What verses have you returned to time and again *(or could you)* that prove satan's lies to be false and minister to your heart in these special areas of need?

3) Gifts for Ministry: What "tools" has God given, what skills has He allowed you to develop that might bless others? Are you an encourager, a pianist, an artist? Do you have the ability to organize, to work with children, to see a problem to a wise solution? Do you know your spiritual gift? Do you have a merciful heart, one that is willing to bear the burdens of others, are you a disciplined prayer warrior? What gifts is He currently developing in you?

4) For Such a Time as This: The fruit that we are producing for the Master Gardener today is in response to His grace and gifts to us. He waters and prunes us to make us better "trees" for the Master's uses. A tree does the work it has been ordained to do, and rests in the times it is ordained to rest. An earthly tree may be a fruit tree, it may produce syrup, or it may sacrifice its branches as firewood to keep someone warm. Another tree's branches might be used to make paper, upon which is recorded good news, while yet another tree might bring joy to a young child who climbs on its branches. Different realized purposes, yet each is important and all ultimately serve their master~man, which God placed over them. Whether God enjoys the fruit of our lives Himself as a sweet sacrifice, or chooses to use that fruit to bless others is up to Him as our Owner and Creator. Yet as our love grows, we will become more willing and eager in our service to Him!

5) Prayer of Commitment & Gratefulness: Once we see God's bigger picture and understand how we might fit in, it is the most natural result and desire to give both our purpose and ourselves back to Him, acknowledging that He is the one in control and the One that gives the strength, grace, and wisdom to continue. Pray, committing yourself anew, thanking Him for loving you, calling you and involving you in His plan. Although initially this could be a spontaneous prayer, be sure to also write out a prayer of your heart to the Lord.

Being the Tree God Designed

"Rooted and built up in Him and stablished in the faith..." Col. 2:7

What if a tree demanded that its fruit never be picked and would never release it to the gardener or others? That fruit would rot on the tree and cause the whole tree to lose its beauty and usefulness. If a cherry tree saw an apple tree and decided to quit growing cherries because it couldn't make an apple, or a pine tree wasted away because the children wouldn't play in its branches, the value in the cherry and pine tree would be lost. Similarly, we must not compare ourselves and what God has led us to do with another. Whether we have been called to do a little or great thing matters not to God, for He is looking for *faithfulness* in whatever we do, great or small. Remember the parable of the talents? One was given ten, another five, and the last, one. The man with one did nothing with his talent while the others doubled theirs. The master praised the faithful servants according to what they had done with what he had given them, not as they compared with each other.

An Opportunity for You!

At the end of this chapter are questions for you to work through and begin to write out a mission statement for your own life! It is an exciting and thought-provoking process, and lays before us an exciting blueprint of our focus, goals and direction in life!

As you are writing, it might seem natural to initially include "I am a student" or "I am a nurse" and see that as your purpose. While these may be specific outlets through which we can live out our purpose, we should strive to keep the focus of our statement on the *underlying qualities* that drive us to pursue those courses of work or study. You may write: "God has given me a heart of compassion and has led me to seek to comfort and encourage those who are hurting." Right now you might be fulfilling that purpose as a nurse, or being an older sister to younger ones, but maybe in the future you will fulfill it by being a mother to your own children. Your purpose is not in being a nurse, or being a mother, but in loving God and following Him as you use the qualities that He has given you in your present situation. When you move to a new phase in life, you do not lose your purpose, you merely begin applying it in this new sphere!

Starting Today!

As you begin to consider the branches and fruit, make a list of what you need to be doing today~ what skills, abilities, and character qualities need to be learned now so that you might be prepared in the future for whatever God may have. Said a friend of Florence Nightingale; "When I look back on every time I saw her after her sixteenth year, I see that she was constantly ripening for her work..." We should see that the things that we are doing today, are preparing us for whatever God might have for our tomorrows. I have a dear friend, Janelle, whose parents had a great heart for missions and desired to impart that burden in their children. Though they were quite balanced in their approach, they chose to live with fans instead of air conditioning so their children would learn to be comfortable in the heat. There were days that butter and salt were left off the table so that they could learn to be content with food that was at times more bland. As the parents made the same sacrifices, they lovingly instilled the vital need for missionaries in their children. At this writing, Janelle is ministering in Russia. Nearly all of her brothers and sisters are involved in missions~ what a blessing to see the heart this entire family has for lost nations of the world!

We cannot simply hope to wake up one day and be prepared for what God has called us to, we must see what we can do today that might begin to train our hands and minds for what He may have for us tomorrow. If you want to be a concert pianist, practicing your piano for half an hour a day is not going to get you there. If you choose to fill up your time with things that are trivial, then you will never be able to attain what you could have been. Although many things may *seem* to be very good, it has been wisely said that in actuality it is often *"the good things in life (that) are the greatest enemy of the best."*

Naturally, the principle that comes into play is discipline. Although, we will consider this principle later, it seems fitting to mention it briefly now. We may have great ideas, wonderful plans, and even initial enthusiasm, but we must also have the discipline and diligence to follow through and be faithful to the end.

> *"Many a young person would like to become a doctor or top-flight scientist (or) achieve artistry and mastery in music but they never will, simply because they will not face the long hours of monotonous practice year after year... or buckle down to the demanding years of hard study. They may through natural talent become singers or pianists of a sort, but they will not pay that extra price for true excellence. They are too lazy and self-indulgent to pommel themselves to the top."*
>
> Richard Taylor

Ultimately, we must realize that if God has given us any talent, any gift, any ability, that it is given for His glory and for the *"preaching of the cross"* to others. Let us not allow satan to fool us into letting God's gifts rot away, but rather be used toward eternal purpose.

Some Most Vital Years

For those of you who are in your teen years, understanding your purpose is perhaps even more important for you. During these years the downward pull is often stronger than any other time in life. If you are living without purpose, then it will be far easier for the world to pull you into its wicked ways. A purpose gives stability and focus, a focus not just on today, but on the future as well. This will be instrumental in helping you soar above the norm, rising to the heights~ and not just that you might be a "good" person, but also pleasing and glorifying to the Lord, radiating a testimony of a changed life to others. And what a wonderful project to help younger siblings accomplish!

An Unforgettable Iceberg

As millions swarmed to see the movie "Titanic," a book was quietly published called *"The Titanic's Last Hero."* Its title intrigued me and seeing it seemed to have a touching, yet greatly unknown story about this famous ship, I began to read. It is the fascinating true story of a man named John Harper who gave his life for many on that fateful night in 1912 as the iceberg tore into the Titanic, destroying this once great ship and many lives with it. John Harper's legacy rises in significance above all others that night, for not only did he willingly give his life for others, but he proclaimed Christ until the final moment he was swallowed up in his watery grave. His burden that night was heavy~ not for himself, but for those who did not know the Lord. Even as he faced his own death, he never stopped his quest to make a difference for Christ. It is told that in all the confusion, he was shouting *"give the boats to the unsaved!"* He worked feverishly, trying to send to safety as many as he could (including his young daughter), all the while pleading with each one to be eternally saved. One section of this story seemed particularly profound:

> *"As the monstrous iceberg ripped the ambitions of others to pieces, Harper demonstrated his unwavering ambition that even death could not affect. He declared Jesus Christ as man's hope to the end. This contrasted with others who were forced to face the folly of their ambitions Passengers in the first-class lounge ceased their partying... the business deals stopped. The chatter of the socialites ceased. But, with his last breath, John Harper tirelessly continued his life work of urging men to 'Believe on the Lord Jesus Christ.'"*

---

* Several times I will suggest areas in which you can work with younger siblings, yet before you will be successful, you must first of all become a servant-leader they respect. If they sense you are only "helping" them to gain control, or for motives other than love itself, it will not work. It's far better they first see and learn from your example. In return, their hearts will become open to the words that you say!

What a vast difference between Mr. Harper and most of the others aboard the ship! He had eternal purpose; they had earthly purpose. Even in death his purpose continued, while theirs became "as nothing." As Mr. Harper was being tossed about by the dark, icy waves, his thoughts were still on others. In his final moments he questioned a man being tossed around him, asking if he was saved. Again and again he quoted *"Believe on the Lord Jesus Christ, and thou shalt be saved"* (Acts 16:31). This man trusted Christ and was later rescued by one of the S.S. Carpathia's lifeboats. He was John Harper's last convert, just moments before Mr. Harper parted to receive his joyful welcome in Glory.

As you consider your own purpose statement, consider it not for this world, but for the hereafter. It has been said, *"We are not here for here, we're here for there."* Though the way your purpose is lived out will vary from day to day, the ultimate goal will not, for we are here to *"know Christ and make Him known."*

Responding to His Gifts

"Make us masters of ourselves, that we may be the servants of others."
Sir Alexander Paterson

It is important that He be able to trust us to willingly, joyfully align our heart with His plan for our lives. Can He trust us to make the most of what He has given? As He leads and guides us, will the life He has given us be used for His glory and for the purpose of blessing others? With us, will He have *"no need of spoil?"*

A PURPOSE STATEMENT ALL YOUR OWN!

"Without a vision, the people perish."

The following outline is to assist you as you prayerfully work through your own statement!

ULTIMATE PURPOSE (ROOTS)

My purpose is to love the Lord my God with all my heart, soul, mind and strength, and to seek to put Him first. Next, to love others above myself and seek to honor their needs above my own.

FREEDOM IN TRUTH (Trunk)
I must remember... (promises of God's Word that are
especially significant for me to remember)

GIFTS FOR MINISTRY (Leaves & Branches)
God has given me (or is developing) some special tools
(qualities/abilities) to use in living this out and they are...

FOR SUCH A TIME AS THIS (Fruit)
Realizing that the Lord has given both ability & purpose,
that the clock is ticking, and the days till eternity- few.
How He is leading me to apply this purpose here & now.

PRAYER
Prayer of wholehearted commitment to the Lord in this
purpose. Gratefulness to Him for the strength, ability,
and even the very *desire* to follow in His ways!

Questions to consider before writing my statement:

1) What is my favorite, most meaningful or "life" verse or Passage?

2) What is my spiritual gift?

3) What are areas God has given me of ability or skill?

4) To which general areas of ministry do I feel my heart drawn?

5) Values~ What five things in life do I hold most dear?

6) What have been my past priorities, right and wrong?

7) What do I want to have accomplished one year from now?

8) What do I want to have accomplished five years from now?

9) For what do I want my life to count?

10) What character qualities do I admire in others that I do not necessarily see in myself?

12) *Who has made the greatest impact on my life? Why?*

13) *What is the most significant lesson God has taught me over the last year?*

14) *What is a specific area in which I struggle to maintain freedom?*

15) *What am I involved in which is most worthwhile?*

16) *What are the specific areas of work and ministry that God has called me to right now?*

Additional Support:

• Scripture: I Cor. 1:4-9; Eph. 2:10; Col. 4:17

• Books: *A Chance to Die* (Elisabeth Elliot) *The Titanic's Last Hero* (Moody Adams) *Spiritual Gifts* (booklet to help you to evaluate the gifts God has given)

Once you have written your purpose statement, take a few moments to carefully summarize it below. Though your initial statement may be as long as you like, it has been recommended that it be written briefly enough that it might be memorized~ making it part of your daily thinking and available for consideration in the choices you make!

She will do Him good, and not evil, All the days of her Life

*W*e were at church camp. I was fourteen. A little guy and I found we had a "thing" for each other. Camp ended much too quickly, but our communication continued. Yet as much as I was flattered to think he would like me, and as eager as I was for him to seek out my friendship in this way, I soon discovered that I really didn't like talking to him so much at all. He had a great liking for video games and this subject dominated most of our conversations. As you might imagine, this was not my subject of choice and I couldn't have been more disinterested in whether "this one or that" had the better bomb noises! Yet I kept talking (or listening, really!). Why? Because I thought I liked him and even more, the attention he gave. I guess I just liked the feeling of being liked.

When that big question finally came, *"Will you go with me?"* I gulped. I had suspected it was coming, but suddenly I was not sure how to answer. I would need time to think, I said. A few days later I turned him down. How come? Well, I can tell you it was as important a reason as it was deep~ he wore tube socks pulled up to his knees with bright, multi-colored stripes around them! I couldn't "go" with him! What would people think?!

He was shocked, crushed. He shunned me from that day forward. And from that day forward I regretted my decision. I had liked him, albeit in a very immature way and I felt horrible for rejecting him. But he would not even talk to me. Ahh, the depth and maturity of young relationships... I remember hating the whole silly matter. It was my first real taste of the glories of romance!

It Couldn't be True!

At fifteen, I learned of a horrible idea my parents had. I spent the next two years attempting to figure out a way to change their minds. Yet in their wisdom, they stayed true to their decision~ anyone wanting to date my sister or me would first have to call my Dad for a little "interview" and to ask his permission. Looking back now, it seems such a simple thing, and I am certainly grateful they required it! Initially however, I was certain that this would mean that I would never go out, that no one would be willing to endure such an atrocity. Yet time proved me wrong... there were indeed brave souls to be found. I am glad that my parents cared so much about my well-being and my future. My dad has never been one to enjoy conversing on the phone or anything nearing confrontation, so I am fairly certain that he did this purely out of love for me, rather than because he was eager for opportunities to talk on the phone to nervous young men!

Although at the time I was sure we were right on the cutting edge of conservatism, I learned in the ensuing years that we were quite far from it! Later the Lord would allow my family and me to gain a new and exciting perspective in this area (which I will share in a moment). We became excited as we realized it related not only to marriage and relationships, but in an even more thrilling way, to life itself!

100% Committed! (well, almost)

It may well have been the Western practice of dating itself that caused me to be more open toward the idea I will be sharing. But here is a little of my story. A young man and I met many years ago and found we had some similar interests. He he called my dad, was approved and given permission to take me to several events. I don't know that either of us imagined that it would go much further that that, it seemed like just a wonderful friendship. But suddenly attraction hit and we desired to be together all the time. Within months, we each became quite certain that we would someday get married. Yet we knew marriage was painfully far away for us since we were very young and unprepared for such a commitment. Although we both loved the Lord very much and sought to keep Him at the center of our relationship, our strong focus on one another was a continual distraction to both of us as we sought as single people to be "fully absorbed in the work of the Lord."

As we read before, this key verse in I Corinthians 7 tells us that the unmarried woman "seeks to please the *Lord,* how she can please *Him* both in body and spirit." I was single, yet could not freely focus on the Lord in my single life. In a sense that prevented both of us from fully being all that God would have had us to be. I remember reading that Jim Elliot once wrote to his beloved Elisabeth, saying "Let not our longing slay the appetite of our living." It is difficult to live in two worlds ~ one being happily single for the Lord, and the other being focused on another person in such a way. For us to have willingly committed ourselves to each other years before it could have ever been His timing for marriage, all too easily bred only struggle and frustration. Jim Elliot is also remembered for saying "Wherever you are, be all there." As circumstances put distance between us for a time, my friends were constantly lamenting that my heart was "not all there," that it was always somehow with him, waiting for his next letter, next phone call. They were right. I felt I was at an impasse and felt frustrated because of this double focus, yet I was at a loss as to what to do.

Our emotional dependence on each other made it difficult to seek the Lord's will without our own will and desires getting in the way. In fact, our emotions made us feel absolutely certain that God would have us to be married, when in the end we realized it was not God's will at all. Yet even then, it took some hard knocks before we were finally willing to realize that God was indeed saying "no."

"He doeth all things well."

As I look back, God's wisdom is evident in turning the direction of our relationship away from marriage. There were some things in my life that I needed to work through, and I believe I might have been a prisoner to them for the rest of my life had I gotten married at that point. There are so many opportunities, so many lessons I have learned which I fear would have never been mine had I married at such a young age. If I ever consider, even for a moment, the kind of wife I would have been, I shudder to imagine.

Furthermore, I would have never pursued sign language, never started GraceWorks, pursued countless other opportunities, and I certainly would never have written this book. It has all been a priceless reminder to me that I must always trust that God knows what He is doing and that He is quite worthy of that trust, even in the midst of disappointment and heartache.

I am grateful my parents taught me to desire high standards and that my attraction to this young man had greatly to do with his heart for the Lord. I am thankful for his godliness and for the encouragement God allowed us to provide for each other during that time. There are long passages of Scripture that I can still quote today, and insights about the Bible that I might not have considered had it not been for our time together. Truly, God works all things together for good.

Fragmented Hearts

Yet to give so much of our heart and our emotions to someone that in the end we do not marry, leaves a difficult process to work through. Once such a relationship begins, not only can there be great physical temptation, but it becomes nearly impossible to protect ourselves from the emotional intimacy that God intended hearts to experience as they are bound together in marriage. Instead of us keeping our heart intact, saving it to give initially and fully to the one we marry, we give little pieces of it to different individuals along the way. Some have even said that this practice can create a dangerous pattern that could threaten to soften a resolve against divorce. Instead of focusing on one man whom God brings, we become accustomed to focusing on one after another. If one relationship does not work, we move to a new one. Not only does this lead to broken hearts, it creates an unhealthy pattern which will become disastrous if carried into marriage.

His Tool to Turn My Heart

Several years ago I began working for a Christian ministry. When I first got to know the others who were working there and realized the depth of their commitment to the Lord, I realized they were truly incredible people. Yet there was one commitment that they had made that I was certain I could never make. But to more I got to know them, the more I began to admire their walk with the Lord and their love for Him (Melissa, to whom this book is dedicated, being one of them!). It made me desire to do whatever I could to attain a relationship with the Lord like theirs. This commitment, I soon began to realize, came as part of the package.

One of the most difficult issues for single people (both men and women alike) to settle is the question of marriage~ who? when? how? and where? As girls, most of us have likely dreamed about the man we would someday marry since we were young. Possibly as we grew older we even sat down to list his finer qualities (knowing, of course, that he would be *perfect!*). And depending on the age we are now, we have worked through different struggles in this that seem to be a natural part of growing up. Hope, excitement, dreaming, discouragement. Possibly our thoughts have gotten tied up at times in this whole process of wondering who this fine knight might be, or even of setting our affections on one in particular. But have you ever considered that God is also concerned about this area? Most of you have likely asked

His forgiveness for your sins. This means that you have trusted Him for all of ETERNITY ~ forever and ever! Yet have you fully trusted Him for things in this life, which is but a breath? We talk about "lordship" in many areas of our lives, yet this area of relationships is often left out. Yet God wants us to be willing to hand over this part of our life to Him as well, trusting that as our Creator, Father, God ~ He knows best! Too often we are quick to look at how the world is doing things and then try to make their ways "Christian," but God's plan is usually radically different. He wants us to be willing to shut the world out and ask Him what *His* best would be for us in this area. Josh Harris shares, *"lordship doesn't merely tinker with my approach to romance—it completely transforms it. God not only wants me to act differently, He wands me to think differently—to view love, purity, and singleness from His perspective..."*

I am not going to make an attempt to tell you what you should do in this area, I am simply going to share my own testimony and the exciting results that have been found in trusting in Him. I only ask that you be willing to take this before the Lord, openly seeking what His perfect, beautiful will would be for you.

A Double Dip of Fudge Ripple

A marathon runner was running through a beautiful city. The course was laid out before her and people were looking on from all around. Some cheered, others gave water, some simply watched, amazed at the strength and determination of this woman of endurance. But suddenly she made a turn to her left. The crowd watched in silence, perplexed. She ran into an ice cream parlor, "just for a small scoop" she said. The workers inside were certainly surprised, but they scooped up her favorite and quickly sent her on her way. She had never tasted anything so divine, and though it seemed to tire her a little, she had felt delighted by this little treat. When she came to the next city, she diverted once again. This time to a bookstore. "Do you have any books on ice cream?" she asked as she tried to catch her breath. The manager found the book she was seeking and after paying the man, headed back out for the race. Her coaches were shocked, disappointed, and with good reason. They had poured everything they had into her, but she was letting it all slip away.

She began to read as she ran. Her coaches exhorted her otherwise, but she insisted that she could run just as well, in fact, reading took her mind off the pain in her legs~ she could run even *better,* she thought. But then as her eyes delighted in the article on double dutch fudge she failed to see the swollen crack in the sidewalk and her toe was caught, sending her stumbling to the ground. "Ouch!" she cried. The pain felt so intense. They bandaged her up and after a short rest she hobbled to her feet once again and started back down the road. But her knee hurt now and she felt the pain anew with each step she took. "Maybe if I had some more ice cream, that would help me forget this pain." She thought, "but this time maybe I should try a different flavor." So this continued until the end of the race. When she finally reached the finish line, she was surprised that there was no one to greet her except for her coaches. There were no newspaper reporters to take her picture, or children that had promised to be there to cheer her across. They had gone home long ago. And she was alone to realize that though she had managed to cross the finish line, there was no gold medal for her, only coaches that were brokenhearted over her sad performance in the race.

Is this not how we often are as Christians in our single lives? We so much want marriage and the very longing of it causes us to be ineffective in our race with the Lord. We allow our thoughts and emotions to be caught up in this one and that one, and use our time to dream about what *could be,* rather than to concentrate on what *is,* on what we are already is certain is God's plan for us. We get caught up in our hopes for tomorrow and lose focus of where God would have us for today. We stumble as a result and our hearts get bruised in the process. I Corinthians 7 issues a challenge to us all:

> *"The unmarried woman careth for the things of the Lord,*
> *that she may be holy both in body and in spirit..."*

This verse seems to force us to take a closer look at our western style of dating itself. Does it really allow us to keep fully focused on the Lord as we move from one "significant other" to another, consumed by thoughts of them as we run this race of life? Is there another way, a better way to approach love and romance? Yes! I think that there is! Certainly part of God's plan for some of us in this great race of life may well be marriage. But are we not playing into the hands of a wicked competitor to allow ourselves to be focused on this in the midst of the race when it is not yet God's plan for us? Consider Genesis 24:27 which says *"I being in the way, the Lord led me..."* What a thrilling thought! We need not run into all the little "shops" along the way, looking for some kind of "ice cream," but God is *fully able* to bring about His will for our lives, even while we are yet "in the way!" What a great comfort, knowing that if God desired for you or me to be married and saw that to be best for us and His kingdom, nothing would stop Him from bringing that person into our lives! If God wants me to be married, I do not need to do the shopping. God is fully able to bring "the one" into my life, even as I am running the race for Him.

This commitment that I am trying to symbolize is called "courtship" by many. It is likely a term that most of you have heard at one time or another, but because there are many different pictures that come to mind when one hears this word, let me give us a working definition that expresses what I mean when I refer to it in this book. It is simply choosing to bypass our western system of finding a mate by the process of going from one dating relationship to another, choosing instead to entrust to the Lord this very important area of life. It is decidedly turning our focus whole-heartedly on Him and the race that is laid before us until (and if) He would bring "His choice" into our lives for marriage. It also relies heavily upon the wisdom of parents (or other spiritual leader in their absence), and taps into the storehouse of their love for you and their desire for you to have a future that brings joy to your heart and to the heart of God!

But how is this played out in real life? Well, that depends on who you're talking to! I have seen it interpreted by individuals and families in countless different ways. Yet I do not believe that the bottom line of courtship is any rule or guideline that could be laid out, but rather the spirit that is behind this commitment, the decision of a heart that chooses to trust the Lord with this very vital area, and is thus able to serve the Lord with a greater freedom than was ever know before. For those of you that are not as familiar with this concept and are interested in understanding more of its framework, I am going to suggest a wonderful book whose author has done a wonderful job of explaining many of the concepts and principles behind this decision. And because he and others have written extensively in this area, possibly I feel a greater freedom in not going into such detail myself.

The oft-Forgotten Side of Courtship!

As I said, though I can see the advantages that courtship would provide for a marriage and the time of working toward this commitment, my excitement over courtship lies in all that this commitment allows us to do *before* marriage! Many of the books that have been written on this subject are written more dominantly from the perspective of how this commitment relates to the actual process of working toward marriage itself. And while this is both necessary and beneficial, I am excited to spend more of our time looking at courtship from the other lesser-viewed angle~the dynamic way in which it can affect us while we are yet single! So although this book is not specifically written on courtship, it seems appropriate to say that it is certainly an important underlying foundation. Many things that are presented might be difficult to attain without a commitment in this area. So let us explore some of these "hidden treasures" together!

We may realize the many blessings of courtship for those that have worked though this process (or are in the midst of it now), but what if God has not willed marriage for our lives quite yet? What are we to do beforehand? Well, I hope that reading this book not only gives you some ideas about how you might spend the time you have now as a young single woman, but that it might even go a great step beyond that and make you excited about this wonderful *privilege of singleness!* Certainly there is no intent to cast a poor light on marriage, for it is what God has beautifully instituted to represent the union of His precious Son and His bride. Yet there are so many blessings to be had in singleness that many never discover until these blessings are no longer theirs to enjoy!

For those who have already made a decision in this area, I pray that this may strengthen your resolve, and for those of you who have not, I pray this will challenge you to consider that the Lord may have plans for your life beyond what you ever imagined! Through it all, may each of us learn to rely more fully on the Lord and know that He has the future in His hands *(Jeremiah 29:11)* and that His hands are infinitely large and perfectly trustworthy.

Our Scripture says that she will "do him good and not evil, all the days of her life." Isn't it interesting that is does not say "from the time that they get married" but rather *"all"* the days of her life. That seems to imply that she is able to do him good even before they meet! For us this means two things. First that we can do the Lord good by serving Him as His bride-to-be, and second, if the Lord chooses to give us a husband here on earth, then we can be doing that husband good today, even if he is still "unknown!"

Devoted to Him

Marriage is a beautiful thing, no doubt! God created it not only that He might fill the earth with generations of people, but also that there might be a visible picture of Christ and His love for the Church. Paul taught that *"marriage is honorable in all"* (Heb. 13:4) and marriage should never be looked down upon as a "lesser" thing, but rather as a special calling that God gives. Again, in writing a book which focuses on all of the exciting aspects of singleness, I do not desire in any way to put a dim light on this precious relationship! God may call us to a time of singleness, and then He may call us to a time of marriage. Our focus should be not so much on our "status" but rather on learning contentment in the place that God has put us and faithfulness in our service to Him.

Since the word "courtship" so often brings to mind the actual courtship process, perhaps it would be encouraging for us to break it in half, calling the marriage aspect "relational courtship," and the time before such a relationship, while we are yet wholeheartedly serving the Lord, "effectual courtship." They are both exciting and important in their own way, and each have unique and wonderful traits that are not shared by each other. The effectual side of courtship is a thrilling prerequisite to relational courtship in that it allows us to focus our energies on things of eternal value, while preparing us in an incredible way to be more beautifully qualified as a wife and mother if God would someday so ordain!

Worthy of our Trust

Many of our struggles in this area are rooted in the fact that we do not fully trust God. A verse I read this morning was so simple, yet held such powerful truth: *"Our help is in the Name of the LORD, who made heaven and earth"* *(Psa. 124:8).* To think, the One in whom we trust, the One on whom we depend, is the same God who created the heavens and the earth (and *everything* from the huge mountains to the tiniest atom within them!). If He created all of this out of nothing (!), can we not trust His ability to bring two people together that already exist? As another verse says *"is there anything too hard for Me?"* *(Jer. 32:27)* Do we really think that we must somehow "make God's will happen?" What a silly thought, that the God and Creator of the universe would somehow need our help~ yet isn't that how we often think? I know I've been guilty more than once. It is a trap into which we can too easily fall. We must believe and know it to be true, that if we are living a life that is obedient to Him, we cannot "miss" His will for our lives~ for He is certain to bring it about!

Such a beautiful promise He has given:

> *The LORD will perfect that which concerneth me,*
> *Thy mercy O LORD, endureth forever,*
> *do not forsake the works of Thine own hands.*
>
> Psalm 138:8

Doing a Future Husband Good...Today!

Ok, so let's say that God *does* have marriage planned for your future (and He very well might~ it has been said that God is more concerned about our marriage than we are!). As you consider our verse from Proverbs, what can you do now that would do your future husband good? What skills should you be learning? How should you be treating other young men you meet? How should you relate to your father, to your mother, to those who are around you in authority? As to your Heavenly Father, what should you be doing to get to know Him, to honor and please Him as your Heavenly Husband? II Corinthians 5:9 exhorts, *"we make it our aim, whether present or absent, to be well pleasing to Him."* (NKJV) Learning to relate to the Lord in a way that glorifies Him and blesses Him ("Bless the LORD, O my soul!") is going to make the transition from singleness to relating to a husband, so much simpler and a blessing to both! An earthly husband will fail us no matter how wonderful or how godly he may be (as Elisabeth Elliot has said, the only choice any of us have is to marry a sinner!). And sadly, we will also fail him. That is human nature. It is vital then, that we have a foundation in the One who first claimed us as His bride and that our ultimate strength is in the One who will never fail us, no matter what.

Blessing Others

And while we are considering skills you might need to develop if you were to get married, think of how these same skills might benefit others as you are single. I will never forget my mother wisely encouraging my sister and me, as children, to use creativity as we played with our dolls. Sometimes, of course, we would play house and one of us would be the mother, yet at other times she would encourage us to play as if we were taking care of children in an orphanage, or nursing children in a hospital. There was nothing wrong with us pretending to be mothers, yet there are other ways that God may use these nurturing qualities that are also worthwhile. In her wisdom my mother helped us to anticipate, even as young children, how we might be effective in whatever role God might give.

Are your home-making skills in need of strengthening (cooking, cleaning, organizing, etc)? Certainly there is a great need for these outside the role of wife and mother! Possibly you could help prepare food for the homeless (who will likely be less picky than a future husband!), or you could take meals to others who have a family member in the hospital, or a new baby. Seek ways that you can use each skill you are learning to bless and benefit others, even as you are learning!

A Solid Relationship

The relationship that you would someday have with a husband, will be significantly influenced by the relationship you now have with your parents. For this reason, one way in which you can do a future husband good right now is in seeking to respect and honor them! What kind of a relationship do you have with them? How do you speak to them when at home or out in public? Do you use the same kind voice as you do with your friends? Do you consider their feelings, their needs, even their "unspoken wishes?" Proverbs reveals so many blessings God promises those who honor their parents~ as well as the harmful results of dishonoring them.

"My son (my daughter), attend to my words; incline thine ear unto my sayings. Let them not depart from thine eyes; keep them in the midst of thine heart. For they are life unto those that find them, and health to all their flesh." (Prov. 4:20-22)

As we mature, we begin to realize how precious this relationship truly is. But by this time we have often missed many years of fellowship that God intended for us to enjoy as families. Think of having a dear friend. Would you not be eager to share all that is in your heart with her? Have you ever ever considered that God would want you to develop such a relationship with your parents? Do you ever work to cultivate a relationship with them~ just as you would a dear friend? He created families to enjoy one another and to work together as a team! Are we anxious to share with them, are we willing to let them be a part of our lives?

A few of you might be saying "but you don't know my parents," and that is true, I do not. Yet I do know that God's Word never qualifies which kind of parents we are to obey. He simply says "Children obey your parents in the Lord." He does not say "if they are kind," or "when they are being reasonable," or even "if they are Christians." God wants us to obey them, just as we are to obey Him. How it must rejoice the heart of God to see individuals seeking to please Him in this way!

I remember when as a young person at church, the issue of obeying our parents would be the topic of discussion. It seemed without fail, the question would quickly arise "but what if my parents told me to murder someone, or rob a bank?" and thus the conversation would become caught up in this ridiculous scenario. Yet all this question really was, was a smoke screen so that we did not have to talk about the real issue. The real problem is rebellion of the human heart, and the desire we all have deep down, to be our own boss and answer to no one.

I realize that some of you may indeed live under some very harsh circumstances~ you may be the one in your home who longs for a loving relationship, and your parents are for some reason unable to give it~ and my heart goes out to you. There is a verse in the Bible that says "as much as it depends on you, live at peace with all men." It may not be within your control to bring this about. Just as there are consequences to us as we dishonor our parents, so is there accountability for what those in authority do toward us. God will hold parents responsible for any ways in which they have abused their position as parents, and you must know that your heavenly Father sees all, knows all, and will use even the most difficult circumstances to create of you a jewel of magnificent radiance. If you have a particularly difficult situation in your home, I would recommend "Glenda's Story." This tells, how by God's grace, one young woman triumphed over a heartbreaking childhood. How in a beautiful way, she came to love and honor parents that were never able to show God's love to her.

As we learn to joyfully honor and respect, learn to bless, we will be learning traits that will strengthen our hearts and bless our husbands. And as we are doing these things, we are learning to serve others who are, in reality, sinners. For just as all parents have areas of weakness, how much more will a husband who has been raised in a completely different family, different life experiences, and complete with "quirks" which we could never hope to change! *(unfortunately, we will also have "quirks" of our own!)*

The decision of matrimony is one of the most important we will ever make. Possibly second only to salvation. Yet satan has woven into our culture that it is weakness and the inability to "think for ourselves" that would cause one to involve parents in this decision *(that will last the rest of our lives!).* Yet on the contrary, involving those that God has placed as authorities in our lives is a sign of great maturity, of seeking to please the Lord and make wise decisions in life. Not only does this please the Lord, but when the Lord starts bringing two together, the whole process become an exciting adventure as the Lord joining not only two people, but two families! The joys are multiplied and best of all, that future marriage is greatly strengthened!

Pleasing Him!

How can you do God, your Heavenly Husband, good today? How can He bless others through you, what can you do to seek the best for them, what can you do to seek the Lord's will? Did you meet with Him this morning? Did you spend time in His Word? Have you spent time memorizing His truth, getting to know Him, thinking His thoughts, loving Him? If you had an earthly husband, would you spend only occasional time with him? No, on the contrary, you would ideally spend great amounts of time with him. You would eat with him, you would talk with him, get to know him, you would find out what he likes, what he does not like, your desire would be to learn to please him. Remember that your Heavenly Husband is right there with you even now. He desires to be intimately involved in your life. As you go about your day today, think of Him as He is there with you. Remember how He loves you, remember that He *chose* you. What is it that you can do to please Him? The Bible tells us in *"finding out what acceptable to the Lord"* (Eph. 5:10). What is it that the Lord Jesus desires, what does He like, what does He not like, what can we do to please Him? What makes Him sad? It has been said, we must ask Him to break our hearts with the things that break His.

A Heart at Rest

But what about my longings, my desires? Though we will be addressing this more in the second book, let me say for now that these are not something of which we need to be ashamed. Emotions, longings, these were not our idea. God created us as emotional beings, especially as women! Think back to the Garden of Eden. God created Eve for what purpose? To defend the garden? To manage Adam? No, to care for him, to love him, to bear his children. God created us to love, and to want to be loved. To mother and to rejoice in being called "mother." To nurture. And we can be confident that nothing that the Lord created is bad. He has given these to us as a gift. Yet just as God gave us those emotions so that should He bring marriage into our lives, we could become fitting wives and mothers, He also desires to use those same qualities while we are yet single, that we could radiate His love and gentleness to those He places in our lives.

We also must be aware that satan would use these same desires to try to destroy us. He would want nothing more than to make us feel somehow cheated of God, and to wallow in self-pity, anything that would make us ineffective for the cause of Christ. So how do we develop a heart at rest? Having a heart at rest begins as a natural result of placing our expectation in the Lord. In Psalm 62 it says *"My soul, wait thou only upon God; for my expectation is from Him."*

Digging Deeper

Furthermore, we should evaluate our true motives for marriage. Some may seek marriage simply because they are lonely or want to have their own needs met. But marriage is not seeking to receive, but seeking to give. So many marriages we see today have sought to find fairness and fulfillment in a 50/50 rule. "I give 50%, he gives 50%. I do half the dishes, he does half the dishes. We both work and I take my money and he takes his." It is all wrapped up in self-centeredness. To most of us, this is clearly a mistaken view. Yet we as Christians can fall into similar traps, even if they are not quite as obvious. What did Jesus say? He came to give. He did not have anything to gain by leaving His beautiful home in heaven and coming down to demonstrate

His love for us. This is the stuff of which true love is composed; the giving of one's self for another. A right motive for marriage should be to selflessly serve another. When it becomes clear that God is truly leading (and that He can use us more effectively married than single!), we can move forward with joy! And how exciting at that point for our ministry to continue as we go into marriage intending to bless and enhance the calling God has given to our husband!

Better Now, Better Later!

The more we are able to learn to depend on the Lord as our husband now and to be content in Him alone, falling in love with *Him*, the more we will be able to bless our husbands, if the Lord chooses to bring that about, and the more we will find ourselves content in marriage (for we have learned the "secret of being content"~ trusting in the Lord in all things!). If we come into marriage as needy women, needing someone to support us, needing someone to build us up, to always meet our emotional needs, then we are going to be dreadfully disappointed. Not only will a husband never be able to fully satisfy those needs, we will become a drain to him in requiring so much. On the other hand, if we come into marriage content in the Lord Jesus, fulfilled already in Him, drawing emotional energy from the Lord and with a foundation of loving Him, then we can truly have something to give. We are not coming into marriage to take and receive from that other person, but rather we are coming to give to them. If they have made similar commitments, what an incredible union it will be!

Not to be Wasted!

As we touched on a moment ago, there is great need for us to put these feminine qualities of love and nurturing to work for the Lord, even outside of marriage. The Bible says in Genesis 1:27; "Male and female created He them." Just as there are significant qualities that God has given more specifically to men, there are also balancing qualities that He has given to women. These were not given by chance, but fill a vital position in God's plan. We can admire the strength and leadership qualities that He has given to men, yet such beautiful, tender qualities He has given to women. Imagine for a moment if all the women were removed from the world. Wow! Not only would our race die out in one generation, there would be so many other things lacking as well. There be no mother's heart, no one with a heart to soften the blows this world has to give. There may be a lot of strength, a lot of business being managed, a lot of decisions being made, but little caretaking, little soft-heartedness, little joyful refreshment.

Have you ever heard it said that the wife is the heart of her home? Truly, she is the one who primarily sets the mood. Whether it be light and joyful or depressing and stressful, the mother has much to do with the emotional state of her family. In the same way, we can have such an effect on those around us. We can use the traits of caring, compassion and quiet strength toward those God leads our way.

Investing in Children

What a joy it is to spend time with little ones! Thinking back in my own life, some of the most significant memories of my own childhood are those of older single women investing in my life (most of whom are married now, by the way!) Even small things can have a great impact. I remember one woman that took my sister and me on a little "vacation" to visit her parents who lived a few hours away. To me, it was one of the greatest adventures of my whole life! Furthermore, knowing that this woman loved and followed the Lord had a significant influence on our young lives.

A few years ago I was driving a young boy across town. There was an ambulance which rushed passed us, clearly in a desperate hurry. Although it always seems natural to pray when one hears a siren, this one seemed especially urgent and I chose to involve my young friend in this prayer. I did not think of it again until his mother came back to me and shared that when he got home he said "Mom! Do you know what we did?!" He then would ask to pray for sirens whenever he heard them. Such little actions can often have great impact on these younger ones! While you are working to uphold and reinforce the principles their parents are teaching them (or teaching them things that they might not be learning if they come from a non-Christian home), you will find yourself blessed as well!

As a woman you need not wait for marriage to live out these beautiful qualities the Lord has placed in you! Certainly He has not "wasted" these traits on singleness! This world has such a warped view of what being a woman really means and desperately needs to see examples of women who truly love Him with all their hearts and are committed to making their ways pleasing to Him. Your femininity is beautiful in God's eyes, seek to use it for His glory!

Radiant in Purity

A question may be in many of your minds and I would like to take a moment to answer. How should we act toward that mysterious male species? The best advice that I have heard on that is to simply follow the pattern that Scripture lays out~ they are our brothers! Those of you that have natural-born brothers, think of how you relate to them. You likely enjoy conversation, but you don't hang on them. You might try to encourage them, but you don't bat your eyes flirtatiously. Think of how God would have you treat a natural brother~ with acceptance, respect and kindness, and this will give wonderful insight for relating to your brothers in Christ!

I have also appreciated the exhortation that we have an "attention to all, intention on none" focus. We should be very careful that we seek to be an encouragement to all of those that God has placed in our paths and that we do not focus our attention specifically on any one. When we have the perspective of seeking to encourage all of our brothers and sisters in the Lord, then many will be blessed, and it will help our own hearts to remain pure.

When we give focused attention to one in particular, we can very easily "defraud" each other. Stephen Olford defines this as *"arousing a hunger that we cannot righteously satisfy."* It should break a brother or sister's heart to consider defrauding or playing games with one who is truly seen as a "sibling" in Christ. If we truly love our brothers in Christ, our hearts desire should be to do whatever we can do to build them up in the Lord. If one only shows concern and friendship to one in whom he or she is interested, or only shows attention while the interest remains, then we are likely revealing that we have risen no where above the world's way of self-centered relationships. Ask God to give you a pure heart toward each of your brothers, and that you would allow your whole heart to be dedicated fully to the Lord so that your encouragement to them might be holy and genuine. Though at times this may not work both ways, what a privilege we have been given of exhorting and encouraging one another in the body of Christ! *"For you brethren, have been called to liberty; only do not use liberty as an opportunity for the flesh, but through love serve one another." (Gal. 5:13)*

Questions:

1) Do you struggle in fully trusting God with your future?

2) Do you believe that God is powerful enough to bring the person of His choosing into your life?

3) Have you already chosen to place this very important area fully into His hands?

4) Is there a deeper way in which God is leading you to that now? *

5) If God were to intend marriage for your future, what can you be doing today that would do your husband good?

6) How do you act toward your parents? Could you say that your attitude toward them rejoices the heart of God?

7) If not, how can you begin today to bless and encourage them?

8) What about your brothers in Christ? What adjustments might you feel God would have you to make in the way you relate to them?

* If the thought of courtship seems overwhelming to you now, would you be willing to simply begin by committing the next year of your life wholeheartedly to serve and focus on the Lord in a way you never have before?

Additional Support:

Verses: I Cor. 7:34; Isa. 54:1-8; Psa. 138:8

Resources: *I Kissed Dating Goodbye* (Joshua Harris) An exciting vision for courtship~ what it is and why it reaps great benefits. *Passion & Purity* (Elisabeth Elliot) Challenges the reader to be content in the Lord and learn to bring love and romance under the control of our Heavenly Father.

She seeketh wool, and flax, and Worketh Willingly with her Hands

*H*er eyes filled with tears as the gavel came down. "Guilty" was the verdict. Her crimes of theft would send her to jail for no less than three years. This punishment was justified, she knew, and would not be so terrible, except that she was mother to a young child. What would life be like for him? In many ways, he seemed to be receiving a sentence on his little life as well.

But then a ray of hope. A Christian organization offers to love and nurture her child while she cannot. She agrees and through tears, releases her child to the loving hands of these dear servants. Sixteen-year-old Terri is among them. She grew up in western Kansas and with her family's blessing, has moved half-way across the country to be the hands of Jesus to these children during some of the most influ-ential years of their lives. I have before me now pictures of the smiling faces of some of these children; Brian, Tyler, Jaron, and Brent. Why does she do this? What makes her care so much for people she does not know, to be willing to leave her family for a season and experience difficult situations with a cheerful heart? Because Terri loves the Lord and is allowing her life to be used of Him. Terri is making a difference.

A Vital Place of Service

What about your life? Within your own home, church and community, are you making a difference? Are there those who would point to you and say that God has used you to make a difference in their lives? What about specifically within your own family? So often we think of "ministry" as being done outside the home, and at times it is, yet true ministry must start from the inside. God lead both Amy Carmichael and Elisabeth Elliot away from their homes and to minister abroad, yet both of these learned to minister while they were still living at home and among their own families.

Just yesterday I observed a little guy of two, who comes from a dear family, all of whom have learned to value work~ even down to this tiny member! The little boy reached up toward his daddy, wanting something to carry. He was just two, but the others were working and he wanted to help! May God also give us such a pure desire and willingness to help, right here within our own homes!

Practically Speaking!

In the initial chapters of this book we discussed some of the philosophy and purpose behind living a dynamic life that rises above mediocrity. Now let's use that springboard to launch us into the next phase of this issue~ how we might live this out on a daily basis and in each area of our lives!

God inspired Solomon years ago in the writing of the Proverbs 31 passage. What a precious gift God has given to us as women in placing this chapter in His Word just for us! And what a blessing to allow this poetic beauty to direct us in outlining and understanding the ways that God might have us personally apply these and other Scriptures ourselves!

One of the first things that we are told about Yaqar, our Proverbs 31 woman, is that she was one who was diligent, doing whatever needed to be done to see that her family was cared for. This verse speaks of her faithfulness, even in the more mundane things of life. There is one little word included that makes this verse come alive with profound meaning. How does it say that she worked? *Willingly*. True, her work must have been tiring and often repetitious, yet her upright character drove her to have a willing spirit, even in the midst of the "daily" things. We too will find that there are many things that continually need to be done, many of which do not seem inherently enjoyable or exciting. Yet work is a gift that God has given, and willingness and enthusiasm supply extra energy in completing a task. At one point I felt discouraged and overwhelmed that work seemed to have no end. There was always a task needing to be done, and hundreds, it seemed, that needed to be redone! Life tends toward disorder, yet God gives us the privilege of cultivating and maintaining order. The following was a great encouragement to me~ realizing that the "hunger of the wilderness" is not abnormal, rather a simple fact of life!

The Wilderness:

> Every farmer knows the hunger of the wilderness. The hunger which no modern farm machinery, no improved agricultural methods can quite destroy. No matter how well prepared the soil, how well-kept the fences, how carefully painted the buildings, let the owner neglect for a while his prized and valued acres and they will revert again to the wilds and be swallowed by the jungle or the wasteland. The bias of nature is toward the wilderness, never toward the fruitful field.
>
> *A.W. Tozer*

Not Holding Back...

As I have observed individuals who had such a willing heart to help others, I myself have been challenged. No matter what the situation, or their knowledge of the task, they are eager to help and willing to learn new skills. They do not stand in the background, waiting to be served, they have their "sleeves rolled up" and an eager heart to help. What an encouragement to those being served!

In the same way, we must learn to be willing! Maybe we feel unskilled, yet we should never allow this to squelch an attitude of *willingness!* This can paralyze us from being effective in our service to our King. Being willing also means having a teachable spirit. In II Corinthians 8:12 we are told *"For if there be first a willing mind, it is accepted according to that a man hath, and not according to that he hath not."*

Certainly the developing of skills will allow us to minister more effectively, and in time we should seek to learn skills that will allow us to be not only willing, but also effective workers. For example, it is important for a toddler to have a willing attitude in putting his toys away, even while it is yet difficult for him to do a good job of it. But in time, he will also develop the skills to allow him to not only put the toys away with a good attitude, but also neatly where they belong. In the same way, not only will our willing attitudes please the Lord, we may find ourselves learning new skills in the process!

Think of Yaqar gathering wool and flax. What comes to mind? It must have been a far cry from any of the duties with which we fill our days! Yet I cannot imagine that seeking wool and flax was a particularly easy or exciting activity, but it was necessary. No doubt, there are going to be a lot of things that we will need to do that may seem humbling and less than desirable, but they are necessary. I am sure there were day that she would much rather have reclined during the heat of the day and allowed her servants to do all the work, which she likely could have! Yet it says that she was a willing, diligent worker. Her tasks may not have seemed exciting, but she saw that they were necessary, and she was faithful in their completion.

I could not find a better example of willingness than my own grandpa. Since you may not have met him, let me take a moment to describe him to you. Although he retired years ago, I don't know that he has ever in his life worked as hard as he does now. Growing up on a farm, he learned qualities that were more valuable than anything that could have been taught in a classroom. He learned how to start a job, and how to bring it to completion. He learned how to walk into any situation and see what needs to be done to help. There is no job he will not do if it will help the plight of another. I cannot count the projects his woodshop has created for GraceWorks alone! He and my grandma both work tirelessly at our family's tea room, and their team effort is one of the key factors in keeping it running smoothly. Not only does their help contribute significantly, their willing spirits bring joy to all.

Important Tasks Come in All Sizes!

We can never think that any job is too humble. We should be able to serve the Lord just as joyfully cleaning house as preparing dinner for a king, for all of our work is beautiful to the Lord when it is done in the right attitude and unto Him. To believe that because something sounds "big" to us, that it is also big to God, is a trap our pride may set for us, when in fact, the opposite may be true. What may seem important to us, may be very unimportant to God. He may not always call us to "big" things. He might lead us to spend time ministering to an elderly friend when it might be our initial tendency to think that our time would be better spent sharing our testimony on a broader scale, or ministering to a greater number of people. But that may not be so. It is far more important that we are faithful in the task *He* has given, rather than doing something *we* see as great. It was told of Florence Nightingale that she "saw little distinction between the secular tasks of visiting the sick and the spiritual duties attendant upon church activities. Into each she carried the spirit of Christ: She was a servant to those in need, whether that need was spiritual or physical." As we follow God's call, our service becomes beautiful in His eyes. Remember what Jesus said? *"Inasmuch as ye have done it unto one of the least of these My brethren, ye have done it unto Me"* (Matt. 25:40). Don't look at positions or opportunities according to man's eyes, ask God to help you see things through His.

What About You?

When God leads you to serve Him in an area, what kind of a worker do you become? Would others say you are diligent? When assigned a task, are you careful to complete it the way it should be done and are you certain to do it cheerfully, as unto the Lord? When people describe you, would they paint you as a willing person, willing to help and to join in the work? We could naturally use the word "eager" in the same context as "willing." Have an eager spirit both to help around home and with others. Seek to have a graciousness about you as you work, which means there can be no air of haughtiness. Be glad to join in the work, knowing that ultimately it is an opportunity to serve your Father in Heaven!

How much easier it is to help when it fits into our schedule or when it seems convenient for us. Yet II Cor. 12:15 challenges: *"I will very gladly spend and be spent for you..."* What does to "spend and be spent" imply? By Paul's life example we know it must mean giving everything that we have and all that we are for the good of others, even at great personal cost.

When you come into a room and there are things needing to be done, purpose to have a willing spirit and seek what you can do to help. At the close of a meeting or activity, stay to help clean up instead of running home so that you can get on to what you want to do. Learn to be a *contributor,* one who is willing to give beyond what may be necessary. Seek to be an encouragement to those you work alongside. Mention a quality about their work that blesses you. Are they working gladly, tirelessly, are they seeking excellence in their effort? To tell them so will not only encourage them in their work, but also will cause them to further grow in those areas!

Givers and Takers

Teacher Bill Gothard has given an illustration about the difference between "energy givers, takers, and wasters." An energy giver is one who is a joyful encourager to those around and considers the needs of others before her own. An energy taker is one that expects to be served and a continual drain on others around. An energy waster is one who is able to contribute yet complains about the work and weighs down the spirits of the others around, thinking only about herself and her own needs. This is a choice each of us must make every day. Will we be "givers" or "takers" or "wasters?" Life will be difficult, this is a fact. Yet as Abraham Lincoln once said *"Most people are about as happy as they make up their minds to be."* We can choose to bring sunshine or rain by our attitude and disposition toward others. As Christians we have the joyful task of bringing sunshine, for we have a hope that can brighten even the most difficult days!

Certainly there may be times when we struggle to be willing, but even then we can choose to have a joyful spirit. The Bible tells us that we are to work *"heartily, as to the Lord, and not unto men"* (Col. 3:23). Often our emotions may not be in line initially, but they will follow our outward actions. Ask God to give you a joyful willing spirit, then go at your task with a smile. You will please the Lord, likely bless others, and in turn be blessed yourself!

Reckless Abandon

Another area that we must be concerned about is the time that we spend on ourselves. So often when we feel or say we are "busy," it is not in the work of the Lord, but rather in serving ourselves. Jesus *"did not come to be served, but to serve and to give His life as a ransom for many"* (Mark 10:35). In the same way we should be willing to "recklessly abandon" ourselves, to give ourselves to the service of our King. While we are limited by time, money and abilities, we must be careful that our focus is not on serving ourselves, but directed toward God and others.

Saying "No"

But are there times when we must also say "no" to opportunities for service? Certainly! In fact, there are going to be many times that saying yes to one thing may mean that you will be unable to faithfully complete a task to which you are already committed. This would result in ineffectiveness in fulfilling a promise you made to another! Psalm 15:4 speaks honorably of *"He that sweareth to his own hurt and changeth not."* If we promise to do or give something we must choose to be faithful, even if that means disappointment to ourselves or "unexpected sacrifice."

A Time for Refreshment

The Bible shows us specific times that Jesus and His disciples would draw away for rest. Certainly this is a part of our humanity, our minds and bodies tire and need refreshment. I have enjoyed learning the blessings of honoring the Sabbath. My "Sabbath," like most, is on Sunday, and there is a passage in Isaiah 58 that gives good insight into how we can make this a day that pleases Him. Certainly there are days when an "ox is in the ditch" and it is impossible to have a full day of rest, yet I have certainly seen the Lord bless my efforts in the following week as I have been faithful in this discipline.

There are many ways in which we might find refreshment as individuals. Some may enjoy spending time with others in fellowship, others may enjoy reading books or watching videos. And while I believe that as we are refreshed that we are better able to carry out the tasks that He gives to us, we need to be careful that our times of refreshment are not contradictory to our goal.

A dear woman recently shared very innocently about the books that her daughter was reading. I was not familiar with the series, but she explained that they were written about an orphaned boy that does not realize he is a wizard and his struggles to adjust to his new family. To her they were "endearing, harmless and cute." Yet for us to allow ourselves to begin to open the doors to the occult, even in "harmless" ways can be very dangerous. Though some may *seem* most "innocent" and mild, we must remember that satan appears as an angel of *light.* Furthermore, we endanger ourselves to becoming comfortable and bridging the gap to more and worse of the same. We begin to feel comfortable with that which God says we should abhor.

Other books might seem most harmless as well. Christian romances for example. And while some of them have been written by wonderful authors, I am afraid that many of them might only breed discontentment as we seek to live wholeheartedly unto the Lord. My sister once went on a 21 day fast. The first three days she was so hungry that she could have eaten a shoe! But after that, her hunger subsided and for the most part she was able to continue on as normal. But if she had decided just to eat one cracker each day, her body would have never switched into a full fasting mode, making her feel ravenously hungry for all 21 days. In the same way if we are wanting to focus on serving the Lord, yet allow ourselves a continual feeding of vicarious enjoyment of romantic relationships, we will likely find contentment to be an uphill battle. There are excellent books that I might recommend for one person, yet discourage another from reading, simply because of their stage in life. Even books written on courtship could at times be a discouragement. Someone once shared with me that she and a friend agreed that reading books that talk about the "courtship process" (now that they understand this commitment) often leads only to discouragement and discontentment. This can easily happen as one's thoughts become so focused on the relational side of courtship, that it threatens the excitement to be found in the effectual!

Music is another area that can cause us to stumble. I was recently at a well-respected event, but was distraught at the music that had been brought to draw in the youth. The "musicians" literally snarled into the microphone, and I could not tell you a word they said. In the Psalms it talks about the Lord putting a "new song" in our hearts. Our music should not be copied from the world, for they know not the hope of Christ. If we sound like the world, look like the world, act like the world, what hope will they see in us?

A friend used to be on call to pick up various so-called Christian bands at the airport as they came to sing in our city. He once shared that he finally gave up this job because it discouraged him so much to see the immaturity, the pride, even the foul language that these groups would use. This is not to say that there are not musicians that are truly serving the Lord, yet the great amount of money that can be made in this industry seems to have attracted those that have no intention of being sincere. Don't choose your music by what seems "cool," but rather by what would honor a holy God and make your heart cling more tightly to Him.

A wonderful test of any activity is to evaluate yourself, your attitudes and actions after it is over. If you see that a certain event, a certain type of music, or time with a certain person, builds within you a greater love for your family, a greater respect and awe for the things of God, a kinder spirit toward others, then that activity is likely one that will build you up as a Christian. But if after an honest look you realize that it causes you to have a wrong attitude in your heart, to speak disrespectfully to your parents, or to desire more of what the world has to offer... these are clear symptoms that continuing in that activity will likely bring great damage into our lives. Should it surprise us that satan would want nothing more than to destroy us and will use something that appears outwardly "good," to do so?

Piles and Piles of Wealth

I have appreciated a little illustration that may be helpful in understanding the underlying challenge of this book. Picture a heap of one dollar bills on your left, and a heap of hundred dollar bills on your right. If you were given a sack and ten seconds to gather up whatever you could, would you race toward the pile on your left or right? Your right, of course! Not because there is something wrong with one dollar bills, but rather because of the greater value of the hundreds. In the same way, there are many good things that can be done, but some of them may take up the time that we may need to save for the best things. We make many choices every day. Though we may feel justified in some of them, we may later realize that we have too often scurried about the dollar-bill pile, when much richer things could have been had. The more that we are able to consider this in our thinking now, the more we will be able to effectively consider the choices we make that will affect the rest of our lives!

We may never know the full purpose God has for involving us in the circumstances we face each day. The true need of the situation may be much deeper, the ministry much broader than we imagined. Other times, we may realize in the end, when we thought we were ministering to a certain individual, the Lord had actually brought this experience to deepen our own character or to purify rough areas in our lives, making us more fit for His service.

Certainly God gives joy and fulfillment as we willingly serve Him! I Chronicles. 29:9 says *"Then the people rejoiced, for they had offered willingly, because with a perfect heart they offered willingly to the Lord..."* How exciting! They were blessed as they gave, and then encouraged as they watched the cumulative willingness of their community to willingly give! What a beautiful challenge to us as the church of Christ today!

One Final Thought

Jesus exhorted that when we serve, we should not let *"thy left hand know what thy right hand doeth"* (Matt. 6:3). We must be careful that we keep our motive in check as we serve. Certainly it is impossible to fully serve in secret, and I think often our simple eagerness to help can be as much a blessing as the actual work itself. Yet we must be certain that our motive remains to serve the Lord, to give Him the glory, and as one has wisely said, "to give others the credit!" It is at this point that our true motive will be revealed.

*Q*uestions:

1) Would others consider you to be a willing servant?

2) Are you just as willing to serve your own family, your younger brothers and sisters and your parents, as you are your pastor or someone you highly respect at church?

3) For those of you still at home, how are you actively serving your family right now?

4) What are new ways you could start serving them today?

5) We spoke of energy wasters, takers, and givers. Under which category do you fall? Why?

6) Are there any activities you are involved in that you realize are having a negative effect on your relationship with God and others?

7) Is there an area discussed in this chapter in which you realize you need to grow? What is it? What is your plan of action?

*A*dditional Support:

Verses: Matt. 5:38-42; 1 Cor. 15:57, 58; Phil. 2:1-8; II Cor. 8:3

Tools: Meaningful Ministry Page (helps you keep track of outreaches to others and God's working in their lives)

Resources: Two Allegories that you would very much enjoy reading in your free time: *Hinds Feet on High Places* (Hannah Hurnard); *The Holy War* (John Bunyan)

Chapter Six
All Aboard!

She is like the Merchants' Ships; she Bringeth her food from afar

"The merchant ships?" I wondered. What application would this possibly have for us as single women? When I first read Proverbs 31 in light of Isaiah 54 it was *thrilling* as this passage came alive with new meaning with the perspective of being married to the Lord. All of it that is, except for this verse! It troubled me for some time and I began to pray that God would open my eyes as to how we might apply it. Then He began to give wonderful insights, so much so that this verse may possibly hold the most crucial challenges of the book!

A Need for Nourishment

God has created our bodies to need physical food. Even His Son needed this nourishment while He was clothed in flesh. But more importantly, our souls need spiritual nourishment. And once we begin to receive nourishment, we are called to feed others. The the balance between these two is very important.

Personally Speaking...

We must have spiritual health ourselves before we can minister effectively to others. It is far too easy in our nation to take what is right in front of us and to be fed on all of the tantalizing things that this world desires to offer. Clearly it takes significantly less thought and energy to fall into an easy chair to be entertained by the TV than it does to seek to learn a new skill or learn more of the Lord. Our flesh often prefers the road of least exertion and we become undisciplined in our living, simply because we repeatedly choose the "easy" route until that path becomes habit. How much more difficult to go into a "quiet place" and seek to set the world aside and all its enticements, and come to know the Lord in a deeper way, to ask Him to renew our hearts and our minds after Him! How often we claim not to have enough time to spend meaningful time in ministry, in His precious Word, in prayer, in memorizing and meditating on Scripture. Yet in the end, if the truth were known, we would have to confess that many trivial things have found their way into our schedules, bumping off what is imperative.

Just as our physical bodies are more healthy if we eat things that are good for us, so our spiritual lives will only be healthy and pleasing to Him if we have a steady diet from the portals of heaven. Many days we may be tempted to bypass making these times with the Lord a priority. Yet more than anything, we as individuals and as a nation, need the blessing of the Lord. And His Word is right at the heart of His blessing.

How satan would have for us to believe that we can reach a state of being "good enough" or of knowing so much that we do not need such a regular diet of God's Word! We become so busy "serving God" that we lose sight of knowing Him. We would hardly even consider going without physical food, yet often we live as if we believe that we could somehow live for Christ and minister for Him without the spiritual nourishment and strength He provides. Not only do we desperately need that daily diet of *Him*, but what an exciting principle He has given in Joshua 1:8, promising that as we allow His Word to infiltrate our minds and lives, He will cause our way to prosper!

My sister spends much of her time ministering as a midwife, serving mommies and daddies as they bring their new little ones into the world. Recently a young mother called, concerned that her baby would not nurse. It seemed that the baby was not getting milk and she wondered what to do. "Have you had anything to eat or drink today?" my sister asked. "Well... no." came back the response. This young mother had no milk to offer her baby because she had not nourished herself.

I once was challenged to purpose that I would be faithful to read the Bible for five minutes each day. Though five minutes a day would be a "starvation diet" in time, to make this commitment forced me to be sure that it was a daily habit. And just because one commits to five minutes a day does not mean that she cannot spend an hour or two in this discipline. Yet vows are not to be taken lightly, and we must be sure we can keep them, even in difficult circumstances.

Nourishing Others

People crowded the busy Russian street. It was the winter of 1991 and we had a very special box with us and eagerly tore it open. Inside were riches untold~ New Testaments in the Russian language. We each scooped up a handful and began to walk toward these dear people. "Eta padarik" ("It is a gift") we would say. Literally in moments, we were engulfed with reaching hands and pleading eyes. Many would kiss us profusely, tears streaming down their cheeks, walking away hugging these presents tightly to their chests. They were crying out for solid truth and reaching out for it. It was an amazing sight to behold. After being deceived and oppressed for so long, their hearts were starving for something that would give them hope.

My own eyes filled with tears as this scene unfolded before me. How much I had taken for granted~ having the Word of God in my own language and also the freedom to read it. It was an eye-opening experience, so different from America, where so many in our country are trying to shut God out. But these people knew what it is like to live without God, and to live without His blessing. They know their desperate need for something greater than themselves, Someone in whom to place their hope.

Likely, each one of us would be heartbroken to realize the number of suffering people that do not know the Lord, yet so often we get caught up in what is going on right around us that we hardly consider them. It is far too easy to ignore the hurting thousands who may be not only starving physically, but have never even heard the name of Jesus in their own tongue. How many tribes have never been told about Him? How many people-groups do not have a single verse of Scripture translated into their own language? The Bible commands:

> *"Go ye therefore, and teach all nations, baptizing them in the name of the Father, and of the Son, and of the Holy Ghost: "Teaching them to observe all things, whatsoever I have commanded you..."*
> *Matthew 28:19 (KJV).*

Does this say "to those of you who have extra time" or "to those of you that have a degree in ministry?" No! It just says *"Go!"* Although we are not able to be physically ministering as individuals in all nations at once, that does not free us from the obligation to be involved. If God has not yet called us personally to missions, that does not mean that our hearts cannot be prayerfully crying out for the nations of the world. While the needs around us may be very real and important, we must never forget or ignore the "nations beyond" that so desperately need the Lord.

A Busy Hand, and a Burning Heart

In order to harvest fruit, seed must be planted, the ground must be fertilized, and the caretakers supported. Of course, it is the Holy Spirit who must soften the hearts of men and prepare them to receive the Gospel. But we must help load the merchant's ships with goods, that eternal fruit may be harvested abroad. Imagine how difficult it would be as a missionary, if your copy of the Bible were the only one among the people group with whom you were living, if none of those with whom you worked were able to study the Word of God for themselves in their own language. And how heartbreaking to not be able to treat the sick and dying people around because of a lack of medicine. Or to struggle to keep them warmed, or clothed, or fed~ simply because there were not enough supplies. These "fields" abroad must be tended and watched over, and if we do not go ourselves, then we must realize our responsibility to support those that do. Truly, whether we put ourselves on that merchant ship, or load it with supplies and support for those who have already gone, there is a place for all of us!

Laura, a former co-worker and friend, is using her single years to serve the Lord by seeking to provide people with the Bible in their own tongue. The need is so great. Laura is not sitting by, hoping someone else will fill the need. Laura is going herself. As she felt the Lord laying this upon her heart, she was faithful and willing to follow Him. She enrolled in the Bible translation program so that she might take the Gospel of Christ to those who have not yet heard. Laura is determined to make a difference.

We must have a burning in our hearts for the Gospel to be known, both in our land and abroad. *"the Lord... is not willing that any should perish, but that all should come to repentance"* (2 Pet. 3:9). Although it is God alone who turns hearts, He often chooses to work through His people in doing so. God will call us differently, but we all must somehow be involved in obedience to Christ, in following the Great Commission. And what bride is not eager to speak of her beloved suitor!

Languages

I remember one time as I was on a mission trip to Russia, I was eager about sharing Christ with a woman, yet there was no interpreter and I only knew a few words in her language. She spoke no English for some reason, almost under my breath, I asked her if she spoke

Spanish. Believe it or not, she did! It was almost comical to imagine sharing the Gospel in the country of Russia, using a language that was quite secondary to both of us! Though my Spanish skills are still greatly lacking, how often in my life have I learned a skill and then discovered even years later new plans the Lord had for me in learning it! Not only will the learning of languages open doors to sharing Christ with people in their native tongue, I have often heard that mastering one language will make easier the task of learning another (simply because we begin to break away from our own established rules of speech). If you learn French or Spanish now, not only will you have learned one language, it may lead to a greater blessing if the Lord would lead you to learn another in the future! Take advantage of the time you have while you are young, investing it in skills that you will be able to draw on the rest of your life!

Never to be the Same

He was working toward his degree in medicine, had a great job and an expensive car. Yet just over a year ago, something changed Mike's life forever. So much so that he began to make adjustments in his budget that he might live on a smaller income, and allowed the Lord to fully change his plans and ideas of what was important in life. What redirected him so drastically? It all started with a simple decision. Mike had signed up to go with a group to Bolivia to minister to some of the hurting people of that country. He thought it would be a great way to spend a couple of weeks of summer before coming back to hit the grind again. But the conditions he and the others encountered were more desperate than anything they could have anticipated.

God so touched his heart for the people of this country that he returned to start a ministry called "Hospitals of Hope." He and others from church have joined together with the goal of building a children's hospital in Cochabamba, Bolivia. Children, even at two years old, are found alone, sleeping on the streets, having no one to take them home, no one to love them. We can't even imagine, can we? Ten percent of the children die before the age of eight, mostly from simple infections that could easily be treated if care was available. Mike writes...

"When was the need realized? Was it after an eleven year old girl came into my primitive clinic with advanced tuberculosis (never diagnosed) or was it after a beautiful nine month old baby girl was brought in with congenital cataracts, rendering her blind? Or maybe it was the children abandoned, sleeping alone on the streets. Night after night I spun a web of feelings and thoughts comparing medical cases in Bolivia with those in the United States. (But) there is no comparison. Children in Bolivia lack even basic medical attention. I was overwhelmed by the plight of God's children, and moved to action. God asked me, 'Who will be their defender?' God gave me a vision..."

One person saw a need, fell on his knees, and said *"Lord, I am willing, if it be Your will, send me."* He and the others have not only begun to benefit the people of this hurting nation, but have become dynamic examples of using their singleness to God's glory!

This ministry of late has become more personally significant to our family as the Lord has lead my sister to minister for a time with the people of this country. When my sister saw that she would have six weeks free in her schedule, these people of Bolivia weighed heavily upon her heart. It was more than five years ago that she began as a midwife, and it is rare that we can convince her to go even a few hours from home because of the continual need she has of being "ready always" for these moms! Yet suddenly she had six weeks and sought the Lord for direction. As I write today, I keep hopping over to check my e-mail, eager to hear from her once again. She is half way through her time there and has been teaching groups of as many as 160 young mothers-to-be at one time in basic skills of childbirth. Many cannot afford to go to a hospital, and even if they are able, many choose to stay home because the treatment that they receive is so awful. Most of the things that she begins by telling them seem like common sense to us, but no one has ever taught them before. It all leads toward the opportunity of sharing Christ with them, and the hope that He gives of Spiritual birth and eternal cleansing. I am so excited for her and to see the way that the Lord is using her to minister to these people. It is thrilling to see that she is able to "teach them to fish," and leave with them information that can help many even after she has left. And even as my younger sister, her willingness to leave her own sphere of comfort to reach out to others is a blessing and a challenge to me.

Supporting Those in the Field

Missionaries on the field so often feel forgotten and alone~ and the sad truth is they often are. They pour out their lives, day after day, and usually without anyone realizing or appreciating their loving efforts. Imagine a family or individual working to share the Gospel in a strange, uncomfortable culture, trying to love and minster to a people group that are far away from all that is "home" to them. What encouragement a letter or gift-box would be to a person or family who may feel quite isolated from everyone they love so dearly! They may be the only ones in their chosen communities who know the Lord, and their first convert may be years away. The cultural adjustments alone can be great. Often misunderstood by those they seek to love, how desperately they need support, both practically, and through prayer.

The gifts that you send need not be expensive. Possibly just small things that they might have trouble getting where they live. Soap, sugar, chocolate, seasonings, possibly crayons and stickers for the children. Just knowing that they were thought of and cared for will mean more than we could imagine. You might note though, that often they are charged import tax on the items they receive. Be aware if this is the case with the country to which you are mailing, and don't declare the "package value" too high. It may be better to send them token gifts and forward money to their mission board instead. Often they may end up paying more tax on the package than the package itself was worth! In some areas mail may be searched and the inclusion of Gospel and other Christian materials could jeopardize their ministry. Please be aware of these situations within the countries to which you might be sending.

We forget, too, that anyone who goes to share the Gospel is going to suffer spiritual attacks as satan will do anything he can to stop the spread of this message. We need to be continually praying God would protect them from both physical and emotional harm, and strengthen them as they seek to share with a world that does not know Him.

Down to the Last Cent

Typically, one would imagine that the president of an organization would receive more pay than the janitor of that same organization, but that is not so with World Missionary Press. And because of this spirit, this ministry is being used of the Lord in mighty ways to spread the light of the Gospel to all the nations of the world. In listening to an interview with their president, Jay Benson, I was deeply touched by what he shared. He described their ministry of printing Scripture booklets in more than 280 different languages, distributed for free in 195 countries.. This ministry has done all that they can to see that as many booklets are printed as possible, which is why everyone in their ministry receives the same pay, just above minimum wage. This allows them to print more than 25 booklets for each dollar they receive. They ship the booklets out in crates by the thousands to nations around the world. Their booklet per month average is an unbelievable 6,000,000. Yet the demand is so high that some wait years to receive them. The testimonials are astounding. This ministry is continually receiving requests for more of their carefully written Scripture booklets. Read a few of the responses:

"I am so glad the Lord has saved me through the booklet that you sent. The second time you sent to me (sic), I passed it around Paupa New Guinea, and a great number of people were saved." –V.J., New Guinea

"I am a security guard. I found your booklet on the ground in a parking lot. I read it. I have accepted Jesus as my Savior. I have done everything your booklet said. Thank you for caring." –J.H., California

"the booklets... have been so crucial in bringing people to Christ... One pastor even cried when he received them for the first time in his ministry." – H.I., Mozambique

Not Forgotten

Do you realize that at this very moment there are Christians who are imprisoned for their faith? We live in such a sheltered world that often we are ignorant of these suffering Christians, and they suffer on, without a voice to speak up in their defense. We have too many other things to worry about, like that person who cut us off in traffic or why our dinner burned. But in Hebrews 13:3 we read:

"Remember them that are in bonds, as bound with them,
and them which suffer adversity, as being yourselves also in the body."

Stop for a moment to imagine if you and I were actually, physically chained together in a cold, dirty prison, uncertain even about the well-being of our own families. What would be our disposition, our thoughts? Would we not be continually crying out to the God of mercy for grace and strength in our time of desperate need? Yes, we would certainly be spending a great amount of time in prayer. Yet often an entire day will go by without a moment's consideration of our imprisoned brother's (and sister's) plight.

"Moreover as for me, God forbid that I should sin against the LORD
in ceasing to pray for you..." I Samuel 12:23,

This issue should continually be upon our hearts and minds, realizing that someday we may be in their shoes, hoping someone, somewhere is on their knees for us.

A Voice in the Darkness

Voice of the Martyrs is a ministry that is speaking up and working on the behalf of Christians such as these. It is hard for us to imagine that in the same world where we live in *extreme* luxury compared to most and can freely read our Bibles and share of Christ, that people in other countries are being tortured, even killed for following Him. This ministry has a monthly newsletter that will bless you as it breaks your heart, making most of your worries seem small in comparison. It is a healthy challenge to read of others taking a bold stand for their faith, something we so often take for granted.

A story was told of a man in Pakistan, Samsoon Masih, who was attacked for his belief in Christ and heavily beaten. He is just 23 years old. After being put in jail and then released, he was badly beaten again, so much that he had a difficult time talking. Though seriously wounded and in great pain, those around him shared he is yet "happy and praising the Lord." What rewards must await these in heaven...

The Voice of the Martyrs recommends five prayer points:

1) That those in prison would know they are not forgotten.
2) That the needs of the martyr's families would be met.
3) That government and prison officials would be drawn to Christ.
4) That Christians would love those who are persecuting them.
5) That God would give new ways to get Bibles and other kinds of help to Christians in restricted nations.

After an attack on their Sudanese Christian village which ended the lives of many, and enslaved the lives of others, the chief of this village said *"It is good for us to know that people do know about us, that they care, and that we are not suffering with no one knowing about our tragedy."* May our prayers, letters (to our politicians having influence), and actions insure that these are not forgotten.

Abroad... On the Homefront!

International students pour into our country by the thousands each year to be educated in our college systems. They arrive on our soil, far away from all that seems normal to them, feeling completely alone. They rarely have even one friend in our country and are very impressionable, for good or for bad.

Other countries see it as a prestigious opportunity to receive college education in our country, yet it costs a great deal of money and thus it is often only the rich and more influential families that are able to send their children. It has been told that Saddam Hussein came here as an exchange student at one point and only the Lord knows what might have happened if even one Christian had reached out to him. And as we hear about the cruelty to Christians in China, remember that many of those in power were once here in America, being educated in our systems. One can't help but wonder if a loving, caring friendship with even *one* Christian during their time here might not have given them a softness in their hearts toward Christians in their own country and had the potential of radically changing the plight of the Chinese church today.

Alan lost his wife to cancer last year. He must have a greater understanding than many of us, of the reality of being an "alien" in this world, for the two he loves the most, the Lord Jesus and his wife, Sherry, both have crossed over to the shores of heaven. Though at times his pain is very real, he has decided that he cannot wallow in self-pity, that he must continue on, doing everything that he can to make investments in that eternity he so eagerly awaits.

Just over a year ago he was regularly seen at church, sitting alongside his dear wife. She is now gone, but her place is not empty. It is filled by one, maybe two or three international students. He picks them up, brings them to church, and then to lunch afterwards. Alan, even in the midst of his pain, is determined not to focus on himself, but rather to invest in others. And because of that spirit, Alan is making a difference.

There is a new generation of international students in our schools right now. Many of these will be future government leaders in the years to come, if our Lord does not soon return. As they first arrive, they are quite eager to make friends. Their desire to improve their English skills and learn the ways and customs of our country are very strong. To meet an American who is willing to take time to care for and befriend them, means more than we can imagine. May we love them for Christ's sake, while they are still within our reach.

Bringing it all Together

Although your investment in others in such a way will undoubtedly help others, I think that the work that the Lord will do in your own heart will have merit all its own. To allow your heart to be burdened by the needs of others will fill you with a sense of awe and gratefulness for all that you have been given, and develop in you a spirit of giving that will bless not only those far away, but also those close by!

As we said in the beginning of the chapter, just as the young mother needed nourishment that she might feed her baby, it is imperative that we are nourished ourselves. Just as we need daily food, so we need daily feedings on His Word. Yet if we only nourish ourselves, never sharing with others, then we miss out on God's purpose for us as His hands and feet. A swamp becomes stagnant because it only has water coming in, but no outlet for water to go out. It is impossible to sincerely read His Word and our lives and actions toward others to remain unaffected. May we be planted by the rivers of water and by drinking deep of His springs, have the strength and spiritual health to feed others, directing them to those same rich springs!

*Q*uestions:

1) What blessings has God given you personally that you have neglected to thank Him for?

2) Are you currently investing in missions? If not, how will you begin?

3) Do you have a plan for reaching out to people that do not know Him? If not, where might you begin?

4) Have you ever thanked your parents for the spiritual heritage they have given you? If not can you think of a special way to thank them this week?

5) Are there others that you have never thanked that have contributed greatly to your life as a Christian? Will you write them a letter this week to express your gratefulness to them? (see page 152 for hints on letter writing)

6) Are there any other ways that the Lord has been speaking to your heart as you have read this chapter?

Additional Support:

- Verses: Matt. 28:19,20; Col. 4:2-6; Heb. 13:3
- Tools: Prayer Journal Pages; Ten Cannons~ excellent video which presents powerful insights into presenting the Gospel to others.
- Resources: *For the Love of My Brothers* (Brother Andrew) *Their Blood Cries Out* (Paul Marshall)

Addresses:

World Missionary Press, Inc. (219) 831-2111
P.O. Box 120
New Paris, IN 46553
www.wmpress.org

Voice of the Martyrs (918) 337-8015
P.O. Box 443
Bartlesville, OK 74005

Hospitals of Hope, Inc.
www.hospitalsofhope.org

She riseth also while it is yet night, and giveth meat to her Household

*D*iscipline. Ahh, yes, one of our favorite words! Yet if you are like me, it is certainly a respectable one, in that it is descriptive of those that are most effective and successful in life. Still, it often brings with it a great measure of conviction. Yet just as those training for the Olympics must learn discipline (though it may not come naturally), so must we~ and the race we are running is far more important than any earthly race could be. Yaqar arose while it was night and went to work, providing food for her household. Because she loved her family with a pure heart, she was able to put them above herself. My own mother has been an example of this quality, being always willing to serve and give of herself that others might be blessed.

We should not be surprised that discipline is a struggle. Even the Apostle Paul realized the tendency of his flesh to go its own way as he wrote in Romans 7. But is disciplined living is found in getting up early or working hours on end? Possibly, but not necessarily. Most often it is found in doing whatever one needs to do, (even when emotions and weariness beg otherwise), though other times it may mean going on to bed when we'd rather stay up and work. I have benefited greatly from a little book called *"The Disciplined Life"* by Richard Taylor. For years I was sure it was out of circulation, but finally I did some investigating~and voila! it's still in print! I am challenged anew each time I pick it up. Let's read his description of a disciplined life:

> *"Disciplined character belongs to the person who achieves balance by bringing all his faculties and powers under control. There are order, consistency, and purpose in his life. As a result he has poise and grace. He does not panic, nor does he indulge in maudlin self-pity when tossed by crosscurrents. He rises courageously, even heroically, to meet life..."*

Truthfully, this chapter is difficult for me to write. Though most would likely believe me to be very disciplined, in actuality, I tend to be most undisciplined. My secret is that I simply respond well to pressure! Because I feel the pressure of time nearly every moment, many of my actions appear to be disciplined. Yet take the pressure away and I am likely to get little done. It has been said that a job expands to fill the time allotted for it, and I can certainly testify to this truth!

We often take our Purpose Planners to home school shows in different parts of the midwest. These shows allow parents to purchase educational materials for their upcoming school year. In preparing to leave for one of these, there is always a seemingly overwhelming amount of work to be accomplished. Yet my time is best spent when I have one of these deadlines right upon me. If I have not been making careful lists for my daily tasks in the previous weeks, here I am forced to do so. Even long undone projects often get completed during this week before our trip, and what a wonderful feeling!

But most weeks there are not such *"opportunities of mad motivation"* to present me with such challenge, so, out of necessity, I have learned to "create pressure" for myself. I might write a list of the jobs needing to be done and how long I estimate each will take. I choose the most necessary task and by using a timer, "challenge" myself to complete the given job within the time frame that I have set. If I have estimated that a job will take twenty minutes, I might set the timer for eighteen. That causes me to aim to meet this earlier goal and gives me a couple of minutes after the timer sounds to bring it to completion. This little timer is also a wonderful reminder that God has given each of us an allotted amount of time, and challenges me to use it wisely.

Some days I will feel the need to work at a more relaxed pace and I will slow down and set my timer aside. Yet I have the freedom to do that because I have been able to manage my time efficiently in the preceding days. God created us to be able to work and then to need to rest from that work. It is a human limitation that He has given for our good and helps us to realize our need to depend on Him. Using my timer is not something I have done to make my life more stringent, but rather to help me learn to enjoy doing work more quickly and effectively. The timer actually makes the work easier and even fun! It also helps me to realize that some jobs are not as "huge" as they seem. For example, I've found that vacuuming our wooden stairs takes just three minutes! Realizing this makes me much more eager to attack all of those small jobs that tend to be left unfinished!

A Point for You, and a Point for Me...

Years ago I remember being challenged to make investments toward my *spirit*. When I make the decision to be diligent when I'd rather give up, to be kind when I'd rather react, to get up when I'd rather sleep~ these are all ways that I am strengthening my spirit, training it to be in control over my flesh. A person that wants to strengthen their physical body must make similar decisions. Though there are times that they might step back from their routine for a day, and enjoy a piece of pie or some fries, they know that they will never reach their goal if they allow these to become the norm. In the same way, when we make the right, strong choices *(even in little things)*, we in turn, award "points" to strengthen our spirit. On the other hand, repeated indulgences into the flesh will give points as well, and as these add up, they begin to usurp the spirit's rightful position. When you choose to complete a task when you'd rather not, or make a decision contrary to your flesh simply because it is the right thing to do, not only have you made a one wise choice, you have also made an investment toward strengthening your spirit~ and against your flesh!

About the House ~ Calling in an Expert!

One obvious but often overlooked area of daily discipline is right under our noses~ in our own homes! One of my dear friends, Holli, is currently the primary care-taker in hers. I have not seen her open a drawer which was not orderly, and one is hard-pressed to find a surface needing dusting. I recently spent some time with her and asked that she share her secrets for keeping their home so tidy. She was hesitant at first but then soon poured out a wealth of helpful, practical information that I will gladly share with you!

A Purpose for Order

She first shared that without order life is frustrating. One is constantly looking for things, having to redo missing papers, to make new purchases to replace lost materials, or having to again research information that has disappeared. Order is an important attribute which supports our purpose in life. Her mother wisely stated that without purpose, there is no motivation for work or order. When Holli's older sister got married last year, they all worked diligently toward the goal of her wedding day. Had she planned to marry just "someday," it may have been easy to allow other things to crowd in, but when a wedding date was set, their energies were focused fully in that direction.

Along with having a purpose statement, it is important to understand the ways God is leading us to apply that purpose now. Just like planning for a wedding requires working through a list of objectives with a certain end-date in mind, so our lives can be ordered in the same way. Holli showed me a list that she compiles each year. It has columns for each project she would like to complete, what they involve, when she aims to have it finished, and a final column for the date when each item is fully completed. She also leaves blank lines at the end for other projects that come up during the year. When she thinks she has nothing to do, she simply pulls out her list and is reminded of all that she needs to accomplish. It also is a great encouragement to her at the end of the year, when she looks back at all the major tasks the Lord has allowed her to accomplish.

Being disciplined is more than just having your life in order, it is the discipline of the flesh behind it. It is being in control of yourself and your actions instead of allowing your flesh to control you. We will begin by talking about taking care of our surroundings and then touch on inner disciplines toward the end of the chapter. I have been challenged by the following traits that are said of a disciplined person:

> *The edge possessed by the disciplined... shows up in many little things. The disciplined person picks up his clothes; the undisciplined lets them lie. One washes the bathtub after himself; the other leaves the high-water mark for someone else to scrub. One plans his work and works to his plan; the other works haphazardly. One is habitually prompt... the other is notoriously tardy... The difference is habit, and habit is character.*   Taylor

About the House

Yes, habit is character, and aspects of that character are certainly shown by the discipline we display in the daily tasks of life. With this in mind, we will begin by talking about a perspective that might lend some encouragement in keeping your own area tidy, and then we will spend some time with Holli, as she shares ideas that will help you to be a key force in helping to keep your home in order!

• *Jurisdiction:* Jurisdiction is a wonderful word for us to understand. This is the area(s) over which we personally have control. It may be just a bed and dresser, a room, an entire home, a desk at an office, a car etc. We then have the opportunity to exhibit faithfulness in keeping our area of jurisdiction under control. Additionally, we have areas outside our own jurisdiction that we should be eager to maintain. We could call these areas of "sub-jurisdiction." Take the kitchen sink for example. This may be an area the whole family uses, and thus it is an area of *subjurisdiction* for you. Do all that you can, even when time is short~wiping counters as you walk through, picking up an item that has fallen to the floor, etc.~ to contribute to neatness in these areas!

Keep in mind that as you clean, you will suddenly notice new things you never realized before! If you vacuum and twenty minutes later flour is sprinkled on the floor and someone walks in from the great outdoors, tracking in leaves that have just fallen, this may be painfully noticed by you in a way it won't be by others. Reject the thought of becoming self-righteous, and with a heart of love for others, be willing to joyfully clean once again.

By the same token, others in your household may make a mess in one part of the house as they are working on a project, and you must resist the urge to "tidy them up." That is their jurisdiction. This does not mean that we cannot assist in cleaning up areas that are outside of our jurisdiction, but we must be careful that we don't become controlling of other's. Holli said that if she sees a bed left unmade in their home, she stops before making it to consider "Can I do this with love for this other person and with joy in my heart, or will it be done with frustration and in judgment against them?" If she cannot answer this question positively, she leaves the task undone.

• *House Cleaning/Organizing:* Holli has a routine that used to be on paper, but is now committed to memory as she systematically works through each room. If they are expecting company she will adjust her schedule to try to clean the day of or before their coming. She tries to focus on re-ordering one room each month instead of having a major spring cleaning effort. Rooms like the kitchen and bathrooms of course need more frequent attention, but working from one room to another has been quite effective for her in keeping an orderly and well-maintained home!

• *De-cluttering:* If Holli's family is not using something, they get rid of it! The "keeping of many unused things" was once compared to the story of the buried talent. It's likely not helping you or anyone else by sitting in storage for years! Ask yourself, "Is this something I have used in the last year?" Do I have a significant purpose for it in the future? Is it something I could easily purchase again if I had a need for it?" We may someday need to buy a new one, true, but how many times do we keep hundreds of things around for "someday," and only use a few in the end? How liberating to simplify our lives in this way!

* *Laundry:* She aims to have personal laundry finished and put away in one day. Incidentally, she is great at getting rid of items that don't fit or need replacement. By hanging up clothes, she doesn't need to wash them as often and "laundry day" is never overwhelming.

* *Mail:* She handles the mail the moment it arrives. She throws away junk mail (most unopened), and separates bills from personal mail. The bills are paid the day they come which both frees her from worrying about forgetting a payment, and thwarts the creation of another "stack" cluttering their home. The envelopes are tossed and personal notes/cards are kept in a box that Holli has in her room.

* *Sentimentalism:* This may well be my greatest personal downfall! I have a difficult time getting rid of anything of sentimental value. *"But I can't part with this shirt, I wore it the first time I ever in my life tasted moo goo gai pan!"* (Ok, so maybe I'm not that bad, but my family would tell you that I've been close!) Yet the more items we keep, the more work they create. Holli said that she will look at an item and think "is this something that I would enjoy showing to my children? Is it something that is a testimony of the Lord's working?" These are wise questions to ask, and should be valuable to each of us in more effectively evaluating whether or not something is really worth keeping.

* *Starting Projects:* If Holli is working on a project that will take several days, she begins it in an area that can be closed off so that the main sections of the home remain in order. If this is not a possibility for you, you may want to find a plastic box for "project keeping." At the end of a work time, allow this box to hold your project until the next time. If other priorities take precedence, label the box, put it away, and record it on your "project list" to insure it's not forgotten!

* *"Little things:"* I once read a book that talked about doing small tasks while they are still small. The example the author used was of placing a dirty fork and plate in the sink when it could just as easily

be put in a dishwasher or quickly washed and put away. She said that we *often sacrifice having a clean home and orderly surroundings for those "little" tasks that remain undone.* Having constant clutter also raises our tolerance level of what we are willing to put up with. We begin to find that it doesn't bother us so much anymore, and thus allow our lives to become even more of a mess *(Whew! am I preaching to myself here!).*

• *Productive Messes:* While we are on this subject, I might add that just as in any other area, there is balance to be maintained. I remember one discouraged woman who seemed more interested in keeping her home spotless than in having a home that was a blessing to her family. The goal is not cleanliness or neatness, but rather to create an environment that is more conducive to accomplishing the tasks that God has laid before us. I could never forget the wonderful times that my friends Gwen, Pam, Paula and I had growing up. Whether it was blanket forts all over the living room or craft projects in the basement, what messes we could make! Gwen and I loved to "invent" cookie recipes. Most of them held little temptation to others, but we certainly enjoyed the learning experience! There are times when a temporary mess will be created in order for a project to be completed. In Proverbs 14:4 it says *"Where no oxen are, the trough is clean; but much increase comes by the strength of an ox"* (NKJV)

At the same time, my mother is a wonderful example of another skill, and that is cleaning up as we go. Not only does it help us find the tools we need as we work, our environment remains one which is encouraging to work within!

• *Getting Everyone On Board:* Earlier we talked about jurisdiction, and here is an idea that you might enjoy implementing into your own family! At a recent conference, a mother shared that she had assigned each of her children "jurisdiction" over a room. She said that not only was it a wonderful way to keep a clean house while teaching responsibility, it was also an easy way to "blitz" the house for unexpected company! This is such a wonderful idea, that I would encourage those of you that have younger siblings to assist your parents (especially your moms!) by helping young ones to get *excited* about "choosing" their own room, and learning to keep it tidy! Be sure to train them in the needed skills, and make a list for them so they can remember all the areas needing attention. Possibly you could switch rooms every month or so, but help keep them motivated and excited about this opportunity to serve your parents! Furthermore, this will raise their alertness to the messes they make unintentionally!

• *Fun with Little Clippings:* Holli has a recipe book designed using plastic page sleeves and a binder. When she gets a new recipe, she glues it to a sheet of paper along with other recipes and places it in the proper category of her book. This has been a wonderful help to her and makes things so easy to find. We discussed how helpful it would be to have a binder like this for other areas as well. If you have an interest in floral design, you could clip pictures of arrangements you especially liked, or you could clip organizing tips, devotional thoughts, vitamin and nutrition research, even for wedding ideas, you could organize a similar book. This certainly beats a complicated filing system to keep track of these smaller items! Entire pages or sections could also be copied and given to another!

Keeping the Goal in Sight

And what is the goal of it all? Our goal is two-fold. First of all, that we might make ourselves ready for action for whatever God would call us to, and second that we would be a consistent, beautiful testimony to others of what God has done in our hearts and lives.

The Discipline of the Heart

Though we have spent great amounts of time talking about outward discipline, it would all be lost if we refused to allow God to have control over our heart, giving Him Lordship over every area of our lives. Although we will spend more time in this area in volume II, I thought we might close with a few balancing thoughts. If we have reached near perfection in these outward areas, and are polished to a shine, but remain undisciplined on the inside then we have missed the discipline of greater worth. If one keeps her room spotless, yet spurts out in anger against her siblings and others around, if she has a disrespectful attitude toward her parents (spoken or unspoken), if her thoughts are bitter and impure instead of thinking on *"...whatsoever things are just, whatsoever things are pure, whatsoever things are lovely, whatsoever things are of good report..." (Phil. 4:8)* then a great battle has been lost. Though in the second book we will talk about developing a "plan of action" for these very areas, I will leave a hint within this book for those of you that would like to get a head start. A significant part of that plan will lie in *meditating on specific Scriptures* that deal with our area of struggle, asking the Lord to refresh and renew our minds after His!

Questions:

1) What are your primary areas of jurisdiction? Of subjurisdiction?

3) Would others around say that you help and encourage order in your home and surroundings?

4) For those of you living at home, name two specific ways in which you can start helping to keep your home clean, over and above that which you are already doing (this could be "seeing that the bathroom remains straight," "setting up a plan for my siblings and me to keep the house in order").

5) Are there other areas of discipline that you realize you need to grow in? What are they? How can you plan to change them?

6) What one thing can you start doing today to increase discipline in your life?

Additional Support:

Verses: I Thes. 4:9-11; II Thes. 3:7-13; I Cor. 9:2-7

Tools: *Household Organizer Pages* (helps in organizing household cleaning and projects, priorities and those involved. *Weekly Planner; To Do List*

Resources: *The Disciplined Life* (Richard Shelley Taylor) A very short yet exciting book that you will want to read again and again!

...And a portion to her Maidens

$\mathcal{T}$he maidservants served Yaqar, yet she lovingly provided for them. Her maidservants must have felt greatly cared for, and as a result that respect was likely reflected in their faithful service to her. We have all been in positions of having others serving or assisting us, whether it was in assisting a younger sibling in picking up the living room, or managing a team to bring a project to completion. Yet have we also sought to serve and encourage *them* in the process?

It is a temptation to view those under us in a more technical manner, focused on their assistance to us in the task, and neglecting to consider what kind of a ministry we might have to them. I deeply appreciate my mother's desire to encourage the girls that work at our family's tea room in the ways of the Lord. She is faithful to have a regular morning prayer time with the girls just before they open. Some days seem impossibly pressed for time, yet the prayer time has priority, for she knows that it is needed then even more desperately. And besides being an important step to ask for God's grace and for open doors for ministry to those who enter, it also seems to serve as a gentle lesson, an example, to each of those girls who come to work.

How might you begin to minister to those who might be under you? I love the term "servant leadership." Seek how you can be a servant, how you can meet special needs in their lives. Be sensitive to difficult situations they might be going through. Remember their birthdays. Be praying for them. Be humble in leading and guiding them. I have heard it said by John MacArthur, *"I can name dozens of teachers, but few shepherds."* Many times when we are put in a position of leadership, we can become shepherds by thinking "how can I not just teach them this skill, but how can I challenge and build them up spiritually and as an individual?"

Training for Lasting Impact

Piano lessons that have life-changing potential? Spanish classes that could change your city? Craft classes that would bring children to Christ? Leading a lost soul to the Lord as you train them in new skills? Yes, these are all possible, in fact, many such things have already happened! Sometimes we miss the greatest opportunities that God brings our way because they are disguised as such "normal" things! Ask God to help you begin to see everything that you do, whether teaching a skill or running to the store, as a potential ministry opportunity.

But how can this be done? Well, first of all, let's take a moment to talk about character. Our nation is crumbling primarily because we have rejected God and the morality and character He wants for our lives. Sadly, one is hard-pressed to find a man or woman of true character in our country. Although our nation has been turning away from God during the last few generations, it is now that we are beginning to see the effects. For many years, although many people were not following the Lord themselves, they had been raised by Christians, or at least in a Christian environment. Character was an important value, one they were taught was part of a respectable life. But as we have continued to move away from God as a country, we have also moved away from His righteous character. If people believe that there is no moral right or wrong, then they will have a hard time believing that there is a God who will someday hold them accountable.

Have you ever thought of how you might help to uphold the sense of morality right around you by encouraging others toward greater character? I am excited to watch as hundreds of young people today are taking character into the classrooms of our country, prayerfully hoping to reinstill a sense of morality that was nearly lost in the last generation. While this is a thrilling ministry (and one in which some of you may even be involved!), teaching character is something you can put into practice where you are. An example that has been helpful to me is in visiting with a child instead of saying *"your hair is so beautiful,"* say *"your mother certainly gave you a lot of her time to fix your hair so pretty."* The first response promotes pride, the second gratefulness. If a girl is smiling, do not comment on her beauty, thank her for her encouraging smile. Instead of telling a child that he is smart, compliment him on his diligence or alertness. Complimenting on something received purely as a gift of God may easily lead to pride, while commenting on God's character shining through encourages them in developing in that area all the more!

Training in character can easily be incorporated into anything you might choose to teach! Are you teaching piano? Encourage your students with a new character quality each week. Visit with them about that quality and then have them complete a short worksheet on it. The sheet might have just two questions: "How can I relate this quality to piano?" and "How can I relate this quality to my family?" Possibly you are teaching sewing or horseback riding, but whatever you might be doing, always seek how you might introduce Scripture and character. Even if it is a purely secular environment, incorporate character and pray for a way to end the class creatively with something more significant. That might mean mailing a short letter along with a tract containing the "reason for the hope that is within you" once the class is over. Sometimes we miss out on great opportunities that are right under our noses!

In John 21 Jesus challenges Peter *"If you love Me, feed My sheep."* It is a beautiful progression~ we love God and then He works His ways through us to bless others. A significant part of His plan for us is that we feed (minister, exhort, and encourage) those that He places in our lives. What a privilege in which He allows us to be involved!

The little people in your own home!

What about those of you with younger brothers and sisters? Do you set an honorable example for them? God has given you a great opportunity to be influential in their lives! Although you are not generally in a position of authority over them, your maturity and your love for them will have a significant impact on the shaping of their lives. When you pick up your clothes, when you make your bed, when you help with dishes, when you talk respectfully to your parents, when you speak words of praise and encouragement to them, know that eyes are watching, and ears are listening and minds are learning from your example.

As a Young Person...

And may I say a special word to those of you who are in your teen years? As we mentioned before, the concept of a "teenager" is strangely absent in the Bible. There are children, and there are adults, but nothing in-between. Now certainly, something magical does not happen when one turns thirteen, and there is still a lot of growing up and many changes that will be experienced. Yet if you are in these "teen" years, it is a time to begin to think of yourself as nearing adulthood, to begin to take on greater responsibility, beginning to contribute more to those around you. If you are thirteen, you will not act as if you were thirty, but you can begin to enjoy and understand what it means to be a lady. The "little girl" is still there, yet so is the woman, and gradually, almost before you know it, you'll find you are more woman than little girl!

There is such a tendency we each have (or have had) as young girls to be obnoxiously loud and silly. Although I believe that there is a lightheartedness in youth that should not be stifled (as God gives us the gift of joy and laughter in friendships throughout our life) yet the lighthearted spirit must be carefully balanced with growing maturity. Often when a young girl is silly, her only focus is to draw attention to herself. I think that a wonderful question that one can ask herself when with friends and family is "Am I blessing others and being sensitive to *all* others around?"

One Familiar Young Woman

Do you know how old the virgin Mary was when the angel Gabriel appeared to tell her of the task God was giving to her? Although we don't know her actual birthdate, would you believe that historians have estimated that she would have been around thirteen or fourteen! Though nothing is written about her life before this day, we know that even as a young girl, her selflessness and purity must have been evident to all. Because of her faithfulness and devotion, God knew that she could be trusted with such a task. When God looks down at you, is He blessed by what He sees? Could He have trusted you with such a task?

Using Your Age to Your Advantage!

Peer pressure is one of the most powerful forces upon the youth of our day. Of course we are all influenced by those around us to some extent and that is not always all bad. If you move to the South, you may find yourself developing a southern drawl or (pity the thought!) putting sugar in your tea! But there is another kind of influence that is not so healthy. It causes us to feel insecure if we do not wear the right clothes, say the right things and "hang out" with the right group of friends. The focus is not ministry, but self-gratification.

How do others view you? Do you seek to bless others as you spend time with them? Do they choose to better their behavior when you are around? If so, what a compliment they are giving! Years later you will look back and be grateful for every moment you rose above what was "natural," and instead strove to please God and encourage others!

In some ways I feel for you that are going through this time as they can be difficult years to cross. But *far more than that,* I am *excited* for you, for as you allow the Lord to be in control, they can also be some of the most influential and dynamic years of your life! It is astonishingly significant to see a young person that is whole heartedly following the Lord. There may be opportunities of service and witness that are open to you that would not be available to one that is older. Often people are more receptive to the testimony and ministry of a young person. While they might challenge another adult bringing up the same issues, because of your age and maturity their curiosity will be heightened as to what makes you different, and may open for you a listening ear.

The world is appalled as they watch horrible crimes continue to escalate. School shootings shock us in a painful way because every year these "criminals" seem to be a little younger, a little more unbelievable. These and other downward trends cause our nation to look for answers. However, when they see a young life that is seeking to benefit and bless others, they will be curious to understand the motivation behind and to possibly seek it for themselves. For this reason, those of you that are younger have an incredible opportunity before you. When you allow the Lord to raise your ideals above that which is typical for others your age, while at the same time maintaining a heart of humility and compassion toward those around, God can do amazing things. Don't settle for being a carbon copy of everyone else. Seek to please the Lord, to be a blessing to others, to be a beacon of hope for your nation, even if it seems you occupy a small corner... you'll be surprised at the results!

When the Lord placed a vision on Sherri Howard's heart (now McCready), she knew she could not say no. Yet she never realized how far-reaching her actions would be. Many years ago now, she saw the need within her school and started a prayer group. The Lord used her in a unique way and as a result, school prayer groups have since spread all across the country. Yet she did not set out to do something "great," only to be faithful in the "small" thing God placed on her heart.

A Change in Perspective

In a few short years your whole perspective on life will change. What may be important to you now (or to other girls your age) will fade greatly in significance as other things take center stage. What everyone else is wearing or doing will not matter anymore. Your priorities will change. You may be concerned with taking care of your family, serving your husband and raising your children to be good and godly individuals. Or you might be on the mission field, consumed by the great needs of the people. Possibly you will be ministering to those in our own country who do not know Him. Only the Lord knows at this moment, but I can tell you that what may seem to be of life and death importance now, will seem to be but a wee speck then.

Higher Ideals in Friendship

There seems to be a great amount of pressure, especially during younger years to "fit in." There are the "popular" kids, those who seem a little different from the rest, and everyone in-between. Might I challenge you not to aim to be a part of any of these groups, rather aim to be known as one that seeks to minister to those who need encouragement! If you walk into church and see a girl sitting alone, ask to sit with her. If someone is hurting, offer to pray for them. And always have a ready smile. Ask God to give you a heart of love for each one and pray that His love will shine through your eyes and face to them.

When I was twelve, and during one of the most difficult seasons of my life, God used Wendy (Carrier) Atkeson in a powerful way. Though she was just a few years older, never have I known more caring, attentive eyes than those she offered me in the midst of my hurt. Though I don't remember a word she said to me during those times, there is one thing I could never forget~ that is the incredible love that radiated from her heart to mine. God used her like an angel in my life, and I will always be grateful for her willingness to give of herself in such a selfless way. I don't know if it seemed little or big thing to her at the time, but I may never understand until heaven the effect that this friendship had on my life.

Several years ago I was looking forward to going on a retreat with people from my church. Although I had several good friends who were going, the Lord convicted my heart that He wanted me to spend time with those I did not know. I purposed to seek out those who were alone or those who seemed to have specific needs. I cannot tell you the blessing I received that weekend as I asked God to minister through me to those who needed a special touch from Him. It far outweighed and was much more meaningful than any "fun" that I might have had just "hanging out." And I made new friends in the process!

Julie was a dear friend I went to school with growing up. When she was a freshman she transferred to a different school and found a brand new group of friends. But these were not the "popular" kids at school, (although she likely could have easily made her way into their ranks), rather they were international students and those who had few friends of their own. She sought out these friendships in order that she might encourage these friends and share the love of Christ with them. And what I will never forget about Julie is that she treated and spoke of these friends with such care and respect, as if they *were* the popular kids. She never once implied "Look at me and at the kind thing that I am doing for these needy people." She loved them from her heart and was pleased to call them her friends.

A Group Oft Unconsidered...

All right! Are you ready for a bigger question? Have you ever considered what kind of an example you should be to adults?! "What?!" An example for those who are older?!" you may exclaim. But it is clearly laid out in Scripture! The Bible tells us that we are to be an example not only to those who are younger, but to *all* those who are Christians, regardless of their age!

> "Let no one despise your youth, but be an example to the believers. . .
> I Timothy 4:12 *(NKJV)*

Why would God want us to be an example to those who are older? Why would they need our example? This is a good question to consider. Possibly the Lord knows what a great encouragement and challenge it is to see someone younger who is living whole-heartedly to the glory of God. I know I am greatly challenged when I see a young person powerfully living out their faith, even in adverse circumstances. To see them making decisions that may not be comfortable, but are right and pleasing to the Lord not only motivates me to do the same, but gives hope for future generations.

Older believers, who may have lost all hope for younger generations will be encouraged as they see your example. There is something dynamic about the energy and enthusiasm of a young person, and when that is combined with a godly focus, what a blessing it can be! In Psalm 145:4 it says *"One generation shall praise Thy works to another."* This does not say specifically that it will just be passed down through the generations, but also implies that a younger generation was proclaiming the continuing faithfulness of the Lord to those who had gone before. It goes both ways!

Higher Ideals in the "Daily" things

In I Corinthians 2 we are called the "fragrance of Christ." What a beautiful picture! It seems most significant to consider that if you were to put on perfume, you would smell the same to those that you love as you would to complete strangers. That smell would surround you, follow you~ everywhere you go. You needn't even look someone in the eye for them to breathe in its sweetness. This is how Christ wants us to be for Him. That we not simply smell pleasant for those in our family or church, but that there is a sweetness about us that permeates the "air" wherever we go. A kindness that is so obvious, that one would notice it even if we said not a word. This means that we should treat all people with the same sweetness~ whether they be a dear friend, or a clerk at the store. One could never hide the smell of real perfume or smell sweet only to select individuals. The perfume becomes a part of her. How can the fragrance of Christ "become part of us" if we are sweet to those we know, but suddenly become pushy and demanding when we are out in public. How this must grieve our

Heavenly Father. When we have a kindness about us that flows regardless of where we are or who we are with, then truly we have begun to understand and reflect what it means to be that beautiful fragrance of Christ.

Questions:

1) For those of you at home, do you seek to encourage your brothers and sisters? In what tangible ways do you do this?

2) How can you seek to be a greater blessing and example to them?

3) Would those who are younger see you as a shepherd they could trust in, or more as a "boss?" What can you do to start actively investing in them?

4) What about those your own age?

5) What about those that are older? Do you seek to respect and encourage them?

6) Does the "fragrance of Christ" surround you during the day? Would those you come in contact with who do not know you wonder of your sweetness and joy?

7) Is there an area discussed in this chapter in which you realize you need to grow? What is it? What is your plan of action?

Additional Support:

Verses: I Cor. 10:24, Gal. 6:9,10; Phil. 2:1-4; I Tim. 4:12; Heb. 12:12,13

Tools: *Character Clues* Though designed as a game, I have used mine mostly as a resource in teaching character! It has cards that tell the definition of forty-nine different qualities as well as a handbook that gives wonderful questions that help in relating them personally!

Resources: Stepping Heavenward (Elizabeth Prentiss)

She considereth a field, and Buyeth it...

The dark storms came quickly and without warning. Water flooded hundreds of homes and left many looking for shelter. But Charles and Linda chose to respond in an amazing way. Yes, their mobile home was destroyed but they did not have time to think about that. "Others need our help" they realized, and headed to a crisis center to help fill sandbags. The next day they helped the elderly residents of a flooded retirement home to move their belongings to higher ground. As they were busy serving others, pictures were shown in the news of crowded elementary schools where people sat, waiting for others to help. I certainly do not intend to be unsympathetic to these, I can't imagine the shock that they were experiencing at this moment, yet what an incredible example this couple put forth in being able to rise above their circumstances that they might help others. Linda said "We couldn't get back to our own place yet because the roads were still under water, but a lot of people still needed help. God expects us to help, not just sit..." Charles said "As long as you trust in the Lord, you can't help but be thankful." Such an example of selflessness in a world that seems so quick to consider only its own needs and hurts. What about us? What is our first response to a challenging situation?

After the storm as Charles and Linda worked and others sat idle and waited, others sadly enough, looted these hard hit neighborhoods, taking the little that many of these people had left. This scenario reminds me of the illustration mentioned before about three different kinds of people. Energy givers, takers, and wasters. Charles and Linda are wonderful examples of energy givers. They reached out~ blessing strangers, even when they were faced with a struggle of their own. They sought to minister to others even during a very difficult time in their lives. Energy takers are like those that loot the neighborhood. They steal not only tangible things, but energy and joy from others. Energy wasters, on the other hand, are those that have the energy, but sit idle and refuse to use it. God has given it to them that they might bless others, but they let it go to waste.

And You?

What about you? In which category do you fit? Are you an energy giver, waster or taker? What are you giving to others? The "normal crowd," lives only to please themselves, but as Christians, our willingness to give to others should be a defining characteristic. In 178 A.D. Celsus wrote a literary attack against Christians. One of his criticisms was *"These Christians love each other even before they are acquainted."* What a wonderful criticism! Do you have a love for believers you do not even know? Those imprisoned for their faith, those suffering for His cause? What about those that you do know? When people think of you, are their minds filled with thoughts of encouragement and are they challenged as they see you making investments in the lives of others?

> *For the kingdom of heaven is as a man... who called his own*
> *servants... and unto one he gave five talents, to another two, and*
> *to another one; to every man according to his... ability...*

After a long time the lord of those servants cometh, and reck-oneth with them. And so he that received five talents came and brought (the) other five talents... His lord said unto him, Well done, thou good and faithful servant: thou hast been faithful over a few things, I will make thee ruler over many things: enter thou into the joy of thy lord...

Then he which had received the one talent came and said, "Lord... I was afraid, and went and hid thy talent in the earth... His lord answered... Thou wicked and slothful ser-vant... Take therefore the talent from him, and give it unto him which hath ten talents.

For unto everyone that hath shall be given, and he shall have abundance; but from him that hath not shall be taken away even that which he hath." Matthew 25:14-30

They Each Made a Choice...

Three servants. Three amounts being entrusted. Three choices to be made. The first two servants chose a path of faithfulness, doubling the money they received. As a result, both were praised, even reward-ed for their efforts. Yet the third heard no praise, rather scolding~ not because he did not have *as much* to return as the others, but because he had *nothing*. He chose to bury his talent, determining by his apa-thy that no good would come of his talent at all. He may have thought that one talent was too little to bother with, or maybe he had other things he preferred to be doing. But as a result he was rebuked by the master for the irresponsibility he had shown with the money entrust-ed to him. But was the master really concerned about the money? I don't think so, for in the end he gave it all away. It seems his concern and disappointment was about his servant's *lack of willingness*. He called this servant "wicked" for his lack of faithfulness as a steward and even the little he had was taken from him. We too have a choice. Are we choosing to make good on the investment He has entrusted to us?

My sister has been given a greater understanding of how much she has been entrusted with as she has been in Bolivia. Perhaps we can learn this lesson ourselves through her eyes as we read the following e-mail she sent this morning: *"I was up early this morning (5 am)... we went down to minister to the street children, and we had to get there while they were still asleep and before they dispersed. The children were wrapped up in plastic sacks, cardboard boxes, whatever they could find. Many of them are druggies and... carry around small bottles of rubber cement, paint thinner, etc. and constantly inhale the fumes. Some of the teenage girls had their babies with them. Your heart would break to see this... and I was told that I had not seen the worst."*

We have been given so much. A shelter over our heads, food to eat, covers on our beds~ these are all things we take for granted. Yet to so many, even these are seen as a luxury. As you go to bed tonight, take a moment to consider that some have no bed to sleep on, some have no roof over their head. Some have no place to call home, no one who cares if they come home tonight or not. My sister said later in her note "How blessed we are! I don't know why!" And I don't know why either, although I have wondered over it many times. Why would God allow me to have so much? I did not choose my circumstances any more than those street children did. Yet I am here with all their lives seem to be lacking. The only reason that I can find is that God gave us abundance so that we could reach out to others, and by doing that, that we might share not only blessings in this life, but more importantly, the riches of eternity.

Those Pearly Whites...

Our smile is one gift that we all have to give, that we often do not consider! This expression should not be dependent on our circumstances, on whether or not we feel well, or if we are getting our way, but it should well up from a place much deeper than that! Would people name you as one of the most cheerful people they know? Why shouldn't they? Do we not have the Truth, allowing our hearts to soar above the troubles that this world puts in our path? For we know we have the only thing we really need. Romans 8 tells us,

"Who shall separate us from the love of Christ? shall tribulation, or distress, or persecution, or famine, or nakedness, or peril, or sword?...

For I am persuaded, that neither death, nor life, nor angels, nor princi-
palities, nor powers, nor things present, nor things to come...
shall be able to separate us from the love of God."

Do you trust God to have a purpose in the difficult parts of life? What is your outward disposition when things are not going your way? What about your general overall disposition? When you join a group of people, what affect do you have? This is an important question to consider. Does the atmosphere become more encouraging or more dismal, does the talk become more edifying or is gossip given greater rein? It is important that we also learn to be sensitive to the need of the moment and adjust ourselves accordingly. What a gift it is to *"Rejoice with them that do rejoice, and weep with them that weep!"*

Out in the highways and byways of life,
Many are weary and sad;
Carry the sunshine where darkness if rife,
Making the sorrowing glad.
Make me a blessing, make me a blessing,
Out of my life... May Jesus shine;
Make me a blessing, O Savior, I pray,
Make me a blessing to someone today."
Ira B. Wilson

When you smile, be certain to give a genuine smile that comes from your heart! Several years ago I was convicted about the superficial smile I was giving to those I did not know. I would purse my lips together in a way that said "I'd rather not smile, but I'm trying to be polite." But the Bible says we are to "rejoice always" before a dark world, to spread His joy about. Sure this is risky because at times we will only receive a frown in return, but here a smile is likely needed the more~ though they might never admit it themselves.·

We talked about being the "fragrance of Christ" in the last chapter. One way that we often let satan have control is by allowing our emotions and circumstances to have rein over our disposition toward others. If you can imagine one saying of you "she is in one of her moods again," I would challenge you to bring this area before the Lord. Richard Taylor writes, *"Such a tendency to exhibit moodiness is a grave weakness. The mature person learns to apply (herself)... with a consistent 'face' in spite of varying moods. The (person) who can be counted on to be... always in the same cheerful, cooperative attitudes, regardless of feelings, circumstances, or weather, will have a steadily accelerating influence on others. All will sense that here is a person of quiet strength, even though they may not be able to analyze the secret."* Certainly we will all experience days of discouragement from time to time, but if we continually allow outside circumstances to dictate our level of kindness and joyfulness toward others, we are not being controlled by the Holy Spirit, but rather by our own weakness. Amy Carmichael put it like this:

> *"If interruptions annoy me,*
> *and private cares make me impatient;*
> *if I shadow the souls about me*
> *because I myself am shadowed,*
> *then I know nothing of Calvary love."*

The Many Uses of White-out...

I made a mistake as I wrote a note in the margin of my Bible, and as a result began using white-out to "undo" it. I diligently went about my task, and was unaware as someone entered the room. "Do you make a habit of marking out verses that you don't like?" He asked. I smiled. While I have never actually taken up this habit, there are certainly a few verses that I would rather were "whited-out" of my Bible. Luke 12:48 is one of those~ *"To whom much is given, much shall be required."* What a sobering thought! Clearly this is not referring to our salvation, for our salvation comes not from *"righteousness that we have done,"* (Titus 3:5) yet we must realize we will all someday stand before God to give account of what we have done. And haven't we all been given much? I know I have~ years of good health, loving parents, a roof over my head, a Bible, the opportunity to learn to read, food to sustain, a mind with which to think, so many people who supported and encouraged me, good Biblical teaching, dear friendships, countless prayers offered on my behalf...the list would be endless.

And even these are not necessary ingredients for ministry, because some of the greatest ministry is born out of adversity. Just as I listed the blessings that the Lord has placed in my life, I can also see many things that I might have surely chosen differently had I the opportunity to do so. I would have loved to excel in school, to be a strong athlete, maybe to have understood Chemistry, *(even in some small measurable way)*. And even much more than that, I would have quickly wished away many hurtful experiences that have pushed their way into my life. Yet even these the Lord has used for good, in ways I would never have imagined! And for this reason I have good reason not only to accept these things, but even more than that, to call them my friends.

Think of Corrie and Betsie ten Boom who lived for years in the Nazi concentration camp, Ravensbruck. Because their family had chosen to hide Jews in their home, they were separated, never to see one another on this earth again. In spite of losing all of their family to the wickedness of that time, they sought to make their lice-infested corner of the prison camp a place which radiated the Lord's presence, and many were saved as a result. Not only that, but years later Corrie was used of God as she shared her testimony across the world of God's grace to her as she forgave her persecutors. Even in the midst of these most difficult circumstances, (which we can hardly imagine), these sisters made a choice. They chose to make a difference, and how widespread that difference became!

What about Joni Erikson Tada? A broken neck at the prime of life placed her in a wheelchair she never would have requested. But once this happened, she had a decision to make. She could sit in that wheelchair and become a bitter, lonely person, or use that very wheelchair to the glory of God. I, for one, am grateful for the choice that she made. I don't know that her name would be familiar to any of us had that experience not been a part of her life. And I certainly know of many handicapped people who never would have benefited from her efforts, except that *she chose to respond with God's grace to a difficult situation,* and thus is making a difference to abled and disabled people alike. And I might add, although I have admired her from afar, I recently had the opportunity to meet her very briefly, and let me tell you, I was blessed immensely~ she is radiant!

I have a friend here in Wichita, Jim Boyce. Though for all practical purposes abandoned by his family, he has refused any bitterness against them. In fact, what Jim is best known for is that he is a prayer warrior. Sometimes he will wake up at two or three in the morning just to intercede for others. Oh, and one other thing about Jim is that he has cerebral palsy. Deprived of oxygen at birth, he is unable to do even the simplest tasks for himself (though his mind is extremely sharp). Yet he has chosen to rise above his circumstances and serve the Lord with everything he has. What a challenge to the rest of us.

Choices in life's valleys

Whenever we are in a difficult situation, immediately we have a choice to make. Will we respond in our own flesh, in anger and in bitterness, or will we look to the Lord, seeking to see His plan, trusting Him to truly work "all things together for good?" As we just considered, thousands have been blessed because the women mentioned above faced such a decision and made the right choice. Though we will talk about it more in the next book, bitterness is like cancer, it destroys us by eating away at all that God wants us to be. Instead of triumphing over our struggles and sorrows, we give satan full rein to bring us toward great destruction. Worst of all, when we resist God's grace, we shut Him out from shining gloriously through our weakness and refuse to identify with the sufferings of Christ. II Corinthians 1:3-7 has become precious to me:

> " *Blessed be God, even the Father of our Lord Jesus Christ, the Father of mercies, and the God of all comfort; Who comforteth us in all our tribulation, that we may be able to comfort them which are in any trouble, by the comfort wherewith we ourselves are comforted of God. For as*

the sufferings of Christ abound in us, so our consolation also aboundeth by Christ. And whether we be afflicted it is for your consolation and salvation, which is effectual in the enduring of the same sufferings which we also suffer... and our hope of you is steadfast, knowing, that as ye are partakers of the sufferings, so shall ye be also of the consolation."

It is such a beautiful picture~ the Lord suffered out of love for us, now He comforts us as we share in His sufferings, and then as we experience His comfort, we are able to become a comfort to others! And at times God may even work through our hurt for their salvation! Purpose to never allow bitterness to take root in your own heart, thus giving satan a "second victory." God knows your hurt and is great enough to hold you through it and carry you to the other side. God has certainly done this for me and in the next book I look forward to sharing my testimony of how he changed my heart and life as I let go of bitterness and allowed His joy to flood my heart in its place.

Choices in the "daily things"

Earlier we talked about two different piles of bills. Because we are only given time to gather from one, a choice must be made. In the same way, choices are often not made simply on the basis of "good vs. bad" but rather on the basis of "good vs. *best.*" I think that the writing of this book has been one of my greatest personal challenges in this regard. There are paragraphs, even pages that have been written and then deleted to make room for something else deemed more important. Other things are in my mind even now that I know I do not have time nor space to include. We have daily choices to make in all areas of life. There may be nothing "wrong" with something we might choose to do, yet it might just steal away our opportunity for something else, something better. Richard Taylor puts it like this:

"If we give top priority to those pursuits which should have low priority, if we 'major in the minors,' if we show 'first-rate dedication to second-rate causes,' if we allow friends and impulse and the convenience of the moment to dictate our priorities, while we weakly drift with the tide of daily circumstance, we will be shabby, mediocre, and ineffective persons."

It really comes down to what we want our life to have counted for. When you look back at your life a year from now, what do you want to see? What do you want to have accomplished? You must discipline yourself to choose the best things in life, and be willing to sacrifice the good for the best. Seek to make all of your days $1,000 days, made up of the *best* things, instead of settling for the "good!"

Refuse to make "soft choices." These are choices we make in favor of our flesh~ choosing to lay our clothes on the floor instead of picking them up, sleeping in an extra half hour when we need to get up, choosing to speak careless words to those that we love. For it is going to be these "little things" that will shape our lives and will give us the strength and wisdom in making bigger choices in life. What makes our lives above average is often just the "little things," the little choices that we make. The "size" of the choice before you is of little consequence, for *"He that is faithful in that which is least, is faithful also in much."*

The Example Jesus Gave

*"For I came down from heaven, not to do mine own will,
but the will of Him that sent me." (John 6:38)*

It would be easy for us to hurry ahead of God and seek to do "great things for Him" that are not within His will. Satan would have us to be busy in our own good doings, but not obedient or effective for the will of our Father. We must never lose sight of His true desire for us, which is to love Him. Our service is then born out of that love. For me to think that the Lord *needs* my help is akin to a two-year-old thinking that his mother needs him to help with cooking. If anything, involving the child creates more of a mess and more work for that mother. Yet she chooses to allow him to join in the work because of her love for him and because she knows of his need to learn and develop. It is by working with his mother that the child will deepen in character and begin to acquire abilities he will use the rest of his life. No, the God who created us does not need us. He *chooses* to involve us in His work because He loves us. And then, He is the one who blesses and gives the increase. *"I have planted, Apollos watered; but God giveth the increase"* (I Cor. 3:6,7).

John Milton, seventeenth century writer, author of Paradise Lost, slowly became blind in the midst of his career. He was concerned that he would no longer be able to use the talent God had given him. In response to these fears, he wrote *"When I Consider,"* at the end of which he realized that all God really wanted from him was obedience. Since God had given this talent, he could still faithfully serve God, even if God took away his ability to use it. Toward the end of this poem he wrote *"they also serve who only stand and wait."* God may call us to grand things, or He may not. He may call us to stand and wait. And what we see as grand may not be so grand to Him, just as what we see as simple may not be simple to Him.

Learning, Growing, Blessing...

Allow yourself to be caught up in focusing on the purpose that God has given you, choosing to serve Him as He leads and to build skills and character that will equip you to most effectively greet your tomorrows. Setting your mind on your goals for the future will help you make wise choices with how you spend your time now and will begin preparing you, even at this early age, for things you likely do not even realize that God has planned for your life on down the road! When you think about it, it is really quite exciting! You may have more free time now than you will have the rest of your life. Determine to take full advantage of it, that you might be prepared for whatever opportunities God may send your way!

*Q*uestions:

1) If you were honest, would you classify yourself as an energy giver, taker, or waster?

2) What area do you see that you specifically need to work on in order to be an energy giver to others?

3) What has God given you that you can give back to Him as you use it to bless those around?

4) What "choices" are most difficult for you (i.e. friends, how you spend your free time, being disciplined in the daily things, having a joyful disposition, etc.)? What can you begin doing this week to make better choices in this area?

5) Is there a choice that you have made in life toward bitterness that you see needs to be changed? What is it and what would keep you from giving the "gift of forgiveness" to your offender today?

6) Would anyone ever be able to say of you "she's in one of her moods again!"? If so, where do you think your weakness lies in this area and what can you being to do to give the Holy Spirit greater control?

*A*dditional Support:

• Verses: Heb. 12:15; Josh. 24:15, Phil. 4:4-5; Gen. 50:12, 20

• Resources: *Hidden Art* (Edith Schaeffer)

"*O*n the supposition that there never was to be *but one individual* in the world at any one time who was properly a complete Christian, in all respects... having Christianity always shining in its true luster, and appearing excellent and lovely from whatever part, and under whatever character viewed;— *Resolved,* to act just as I would do, if I strove with all my might *to be that one,* who should live in my time."

Jonathan Edwards

With the fruit of her hands She Planteth a Vineyard

*I*magine that a man started a business, and in time, it became very profitable. It made millions of dollars each year. Though its success was largely due to the work of another, the man never thanked his colleague, in fact, he did not even do anything with the money. Instead he buried it in his backyard and furthermore, applied for welfare and began to live off of money intended for those in desperate need. What would you think of such a man?

"How selfish!" And yes, it really is, but aren't we often are guilty of the same thing ourselves? We have been raised in a country that was founded upon the Bible. Many of us were brought up in Christian homes by parents who were up with us at 3 am when we got sick, who nurtured us as we grew, who taught us the things of the Lord. Yet often we bury the treasure that we have been given to bless others, continuing instead to take from those around us.

As the parable in the previous chapter spoke of talents, so we too have been given similar "talents" for the use of the kingdom. Though it may be easy to look at someone else and think we could do great things if we only had their talent, that is not what God is asking of us. He is simply asking us to be faithful with what we *have* been given.

It has been said that that there are three ways to give and invest in others and we each have been given something of great worth to invest. They have been categorized as "time, talent, and treasure." Some people are born with great talent. It may be musical, an ability to organize, a skill of speaking to large groups of people, or being a great cook. Others may not feel so gifted in any certain area, but they may have the gift of time that they can give. They may be able to do volunteer work, or minister to a family experiencing some struggles~ cleaning house for them or taking care of their children. Others may have the gift of treasure. They are able to financially support others whether it be a ministry or a poor family. Others may have treasure in their closets and can give warm clothes to needy people in the winter or contribute in others ways. Never think that you have nothing to give. You have much more than you know.

Worthy Investments

When we give to others, it is like an investment. Yet there are so many causes, so many needy people, so many "good" organizations. We could never give to all. So what is a worthy investment of our lives? That is something you will have to ask the Lord to answer for you. He may lead you in many different ways. But it is necessary that we not just be busy doing "good" things. Certainly there are times when the Lord will simply call us to clean someone's home, or take out their trash. These jobs, done in a loving way, may open a door of ministry with someone the Lord has laid on our heart. But we must always consider whether what we are doing is going to matter in eternity. If we allow our focus to be on these "good" things, there is great danger that we will become comfortable there, forgetting to acknowledge to others the true source of that goodness.

Living Examples

There was a question that Bill Gothard asked himself when he entered high school. This question radically changed his focus in life.

"Will this matter for eternity?" he thought as he considered each new opportunity. Of course, he did not quit doing his chores or completing his homework (as these were still a part of daily life and important for maintaining a good testimony), but instead of involving himself in all of the "normal" activities of his classmates, he busied himself in serving others for the cause of Christ. He designed evangelical birthday cards for each one of his classmates, and thought of new projects every year that might bless those around him. Yes, people around him thought he was different. But they did not scorn or mock him, rather they held him in high esteem. Why? Because they knew that he *sincerely loved them* and they could see the sacrifice that he was making on their behalf. In fact, at his graduation he was lovingly presented with a sizable scholarship from his classmates in response to his concern. He used his time to make lasting investments that he will never regret.

❧

A similar question fought against the hearts and minds of twin sisters Terri and Tracy. Gifted athletically, and a vital part of their school basketball team, the Lord placed a burden on their hearts for their classmates who did not know the Lord and how little time they had left. The decision was made. They knew the Lord was leading them to quit the team. Possibly God would allow other Christians on the team to stay, but these sisters could not deny God's call. They respectfully asked to be pulled from the team and despite their coach entreating them to reconsider, they remained faithful to their call.

And not only did they quit the team, they carefully initiated a plan of action. As sisters, they started a Bible study on campus that had a specific plan to edify and challenge each member. As a result they saw amazing things happen in their high school, and an incredible number of their friends were saved as the Lord worked through their efforts. Would they say that the sacrifice was too great? No, of course not, they would do it again in a moment. These sisters chose not to live "normal" lives, they chose to make a difference.

Melissa Perry chose to make a difference in the lives of those around her simply by putting the needs of others above herself and by her willingness to "be spent" as she gave wholeheartedly to others. As a result, she has been one that the Lord worked through to touch and challenge countless individuals. I just happen to be one of them. Full of kindness and love, she poured herself into each person she met. I don't believe that she ever once considered "what is in this for me?" as she continually blessed those around her. When I first met Melissa, I was facing a time of struggle in seeking to understand God's plan for my life. Some difficult things had happened that seemed to take the floor right out from under me. I cannot count the hours of conversation that we shared, nor the tears I shed in some of them, but the investment she made in me, and her radiance for the Lord challenged me to desire to seek Him in a way I never had before.

When I think of her today (many miles separate us now), I primarily remember three things. First of all that she had a deeply personal relationship with the Lord and spent great amounts of time getting to know Him and meditating upon His Word. Second, I remember her laugh! It was so joyful and had a way of making everyone feel warmly accepted and loved of her. And thirdly, I remember her attentiveness to the needs and hurts of others, the way that her eyes told that she was vicariously experiencing the same hurt or sorrow being shared, and the wisdom she had as she would respond (certainly the result of her deep relationship with Christ). Although God has used many individuals to teach me His ways and character throughout the years, He used Melissa in a way she will never know, to shape my life and to inspire my heart. Much of the vision in this book was planted in my heart as she willingly lived it out before me. It is for this reason I have dedicated it to her. I love you, Melis.

Knowing God's Will

But how can one be certain she is within God's will? First of all, God is not trying to hide His will for His children. Of course, our own disobedience can block His will from being clear to us. If we are living in disobedience to Him in one area, and have closed our ears to Him, we cannot expect to hear Him very well in others. But if we have hearts that are seeking to please and follow Him, He will surely lead. He may not give us a map that shows as much territory ahead as we would like, but He will show us the next step. As it says in Psalm 119:105; *"Thy word is a lamp unto my feet, and a light unto my path."* Ask Him to show you the next step, and while you focus on stepping, trust Him for the one beyond that. Like a child who is dependent on a parent for daily food and care, so we are daily dependent upon the Lord. It was once said "Our need is the most glorious possession we have outside of Christ Himself." What a beautiful perspective! It is not abundance or ease that keeps us returning to the throne of grace, but rather our great need of Him and the grace which He offers.

Firm Foundation

Our service to Him will never be possible without a solid foundation. In ourselves, we could never have the strength, wisdom or even the willingness to follow His will. If we wish to have a lasting impact on this world, we must first be certain that our foundation is strong. If I wanted to put a small shed in my backyard, I would not need much of a foundation. In fact, years ago we had a dog named April, and there was no foundation whatsoever under her little house. But if one was building a big, glorious structure, then it would be vital that the foundation would run deep. An architect could design a beautiful skyscraper, but if he had not also planned a deep, strong foundation, the building will soon crack and fall, endangering the lives of many. When we look at a skyline of a city it often seems powerful and awesome, but what our eyes cannot see is the foundation that gives those buildings the ability to stand. No work can be done on the visible parts of a building until the foundation is in place. In the same way, we cannot hope to serve God in great ways until we allow Him to dig a deep foundation in our lives, which may never be seen by human eyes. Yet as that foundation is deepened, He is able to build upon it for His glory.

So what must be the foundation of our service to Him? There is only one foundation, the Lord Jesus Christ. He lays and deepens that foundation of *Him* in our lives as we allow Him to infiltrate our mind, soul, heart and strength. This happens when our heart, our thoughts, our goals, our *everything* is centered upon Him.

> *"According to the grace of God ..*
> *I have laid the foundation, and another buildeth thereon.*
> *But let every man take heed how he buildeth thereupon.*
> *For other foundation can no man lay*
> *than that is laid, which is Jesus Christ.*
> *Now if any man build upon this foundation*
> *gold, silver, precious stones, wood, hay, stubble;*
> *Every man's work shall be made manifest:*
> *for the day shall declare it, because it shall be revealed by fire;*
> *and the fire shall try every man's work*
> *of what sort it is. If any man's work abide*
> *which he hath built thereupon, he shall receive a reward."*
>
> I Cor. 3:8-15

Quite a strong passage. Clearly, although our salvation is not at stake, what we produce for Him upon that foundation is not a trivial matter. Dr. N.A. Woychuk has written a book, *"Building Gold, Silver, and Precious Stones,"* which is devoted to the study of this passage.

In this book, he likens:

Gold, to "personal, direct, conscious communion with God,"

Silver, to fellowship with other believers (founded upon the gold,
"if we walk in the light, as He is in the light, we have fellowship one with another..." 1 John 1:7)

Precious Stones, to opportunities in witnessing to non-Christians

The order of these three is no accident. The foundation of our lives on the Lord Jesus Christ gives us a basis from which we can minister to others. If our hearts are not pure toward other Christians (the silver) we cannot effectively witness to others. For how can we love those that do not share our fellowship with the Lord, if our hearts are not pure and loving toward our brothers and sisters in Christ?

Do you have both Christian and non-Christian friends? So often as Christians we enjoy the fellowship of one another so much that we neglect to reach out. Of course our relationships will be different with those yet outside the faith. We can have close, personal friendships with those that share our love for the Lord, while those that do not know Him are our "mission field." We must be sure that we are influencing them toward the Lord instead of them influencing us away from Him. Unless you are older and very mature, I would hesitate to encourage you to spend great amounts of time with someone who is not saved. You might ask your parents for counsel. There are many opportunities that you could enjoy as a family, such as ministering to neighbors that do not know the Lord, or witnessing at care homes. I issue this caution because I have seen too many young people drawn away from the Lord simply because they chose the wrong friends, often in hopes of "witnessing." When you are older, the risk lessens and God may give other opportunities. For now, use careful discretion, but have an open heart to witness to others that God brings your way.

Multiplying Your "Millions"

Just as the man with the buried treasure will never see his millions multiplied, we will never reap from what we have been given unless we are willing to invest it in others. As we develop true, selfless love for those whom God has placed around us who know Him, it will be a natural outflowing to want to reach others who are yet outside the flock. As they watch our lives, may they also desire the beauty of the "gold," and the blessing and encouragement that is found in the "silver!"

This cycle will not end with you! For as you invest in others, they will have the opportunity to invest themselves in someone else. Whenever we invest in others, we must always keep this in view. What an encouragement it can be! It has been said (for example), that if we counsel others, we should never imagine that our purpose lies solely in helping them, but also in building them up in the Lord that they themselves might continue in ministry to others.

What does God Require?

Some of you may be wishing you had something "great" to invest. I can understand this feeling quite well. I remember praying when I must have been thirteen or so, that God would allow me to do just *one thing* well. It seemed as if talent abounded about me, but none was within. I was certain I was a failure.

But what is talent? We rarely see God looking for talent in Scripture. The only time that comes immediately to mind was when the tabernacle was being built, but even then, they came and were inspired of God in their work *("... every wise hearted man, in whom the LORD put wisdom and understanding to know how to work..." Ex. 36:1)*. No, in the Bible we see God looking for righteousness, for holiness, for seeking after Him, but rarely for talent. Remember Moses? God wanted him to be His voice before Pharaoh on behalf of the Israelites. Was Moses chosen because of his excellent oratory skills? Certainly not! This of all areas was not a realm of strength for him. Moses reminded the Lord of his slow tongue, yet the Lord reminded Moses of His all-sufficiency. *"I will be with thine mouth and teach thee what thou shalt say" (Ex. 4:12)*.

God does not require talent, in fact, many times He chooses to work *through* our *weaknesses*~ they are never a limit to Him! II Corinthians 12:9 says *"My grace is sufficient for thee; for My strength is made perfect in weakness. Most gladly therefore will I rather glory in my infirmities, that the power of Christ may rest upon me."* What a glorious promise! It is our very weakness that makes possible (and visible!) the power of Christ in our lives! When our lives testify of His power and strength despite our own weakness, and when met with struggles and trials, we respond with hope instead of bitterness and self pity, the world is forced to acknowledge that something greater, something supernatural is at work.

If we feel we have little talent, yet the Lord chooses to use our small sack of "loaves and fishes" for His glory, then *He* is clearly the multiplier, not we ourselves. There was no doubt in anyone's mind as to who provided the food for the thousands that day. It was God who provided, yet how precious that He chose to work through a poor child who had hardly anything to offer, hardly anything except that which really mattered~ the willingness to offer what little he had.

We also read about David. Was he chosen for his greatness? No, he was the least logical to be chosen of all of his brothers. In fact, when Samuel was led of God to Jesse's family to choose God's anointed, David was so unlikely, he was not even brought in for review! Where was he? In the fields, tending sheep, being faithful to a call that could not have been very glorious, yet it was the task he was given to perform. God knew just when to bring him out, knowing that the things he was learning there in the pasture, all alone, were exactly the lessons that were necessary for the position God would give him later in life. And what was that position? Killing giants, becoming king, and finally being part of the lineage of Christ! No small tasks! Yet in all of this, where was his focus? On the Lord. Let's read a few verses from this powerful story.

> *"And Saul said to David, 'You are not able to go against this Philistine to fight with him, for you are a youth, and he a man of war from his youth.' But David said to Saul, 'Your servant used to keep his father's sheep, and when a lion... came... I went out after it and struck it, and delivered the lamb from its mouth; and ... killed it. Your servant has killed both lion and bear; and this uncircumcised Philistine will be like one of them, seeing he has defiled the armies of the living God... 'The LORD who delivered me from the paw of the lion... He will deliver me out from the hand of the Philistine.'"*
>
> 1 Samuel 17:33-36 (NKJV)

David realized that God had given him a skill and he had developed it excellently. Yet he also knew that it was God who worked through that skill to give victory. His strength was in the Lord, and his equipment was the skills that God had taught him during monotonous hours of tending sheep. His only choice was to trust in God and in what He had given.

An Oft-Forgotten Key

I have heard it said that satan pays little attention to our strivings, our efforts, but *trembles* when we are on our knees. We have such a little ability to comprehend the spiritual battles that take place within the heavenlies~ it is so easy for us to lose sight of this "greater battle" going on. Satan trembles because there is power in prayer and he knows that his kingdom will be damaged greatly by it. He trembles because he knows that God mysteriously uses prayer to turn hearts toward Him and accomplish His will on the earth. If only we "knew" this ourselves! I think that when we arrive in heaven we will have great regrets at our loss in this area. Additionally, we can do many "wonderful" things for God, but without His initial leading to do them, and empowerment as they are in progress, they are little more than works of the flesh that will have no lasting value. *"Unless the Lord builds the house, they labor in vain who build it..."* (Psa. 127:1)

God Uses Our Nothingness When Given to Him

Will you allow me to share a personal story that demonstrates the way God desires to work, even through the weakness in our lives? As I look back and remember my prayer to be "good at one thing" I see that it was never God's highest goal for me to be "good" at something but rather that I might seek to glorify Him and edify others.

When I was 14, I met a girl named Tammy. She was about my age and though bubbly, seemed lonely. I saw her weekly as our families would both eat at the same restaurant after church. As much as I desired to get to know her, there was a great barrier between us. Tammy was deaf. The only way that we could converse was through her mother. After several months, I finally decided to try to learn her language. I enrolled in a sign language class and practiced for hours each week, trying to gain the nerve to actually "say" something to her! I will never forget the first time I approached her to say "hello" in this language that was still so strange to me. My greatest fear was that she might "talk" back to me, and sure enough she did (and of course I had no idea what she said!). Yet she was very patient with me and helped me during our weekly visits.

I went to a church camp the next summer and was surprised to find two deaf campers among our group. I was terribly shy, but felt guilty not welcoming them. Finally I greeted them in "broken" and shaking sign. "Whew! Duty done!" I thought. Yet I realized my relief was short-lived, as they approached me the next morning to ask if I could interpret for them. Now let me tell you, I was no more ready to interpret than I was prepared to train an elephant for the circus! I tried to explain this to them, but they persisted. To me this was a great struggle. I had gone to camp to be ministered unto and to have fun with my friends, not to have to serve others. Furthermore, what would my friends think? To sit up front and attempt to perform a skill in which I was far from being adept seemed most humiliating. Yet in the midst of my great immaturity, God was wanting to stretch me. I survived the week, and God taught me lessons I desperately needed to learn. I must say by the end though, I was certain I would never sign another word in my life!

Yet God was not finished. I would see deaf people in stores needing help, or assistance in other places. I never sought to "interpret," but it seemed God was placing this in my path. The more deaf individuals I met, the more God would lay it on my heart to minister to them. As I began to understand the mysteries of this beautiful language, the Lord opened the door for ministry as an interpreter in our area.

Years later I met a friend of Tammy's who was also deaf. Because of poor choices and a few hard knocks, he was experiencing many struggles and great discouragement. As we talked, I was able to share the Gospel, that Jesus had come to pay the penalty for his sins. The Lord softened his heart that day, and with tears he prayed a precious prayer, receiving Christ's forgiveness and salvation. Could I ever have imagined this when I took that first class? No, but God certainly had.

After a couple of years of teaching sign language to children, I began to incorporate both character and Scripture into the classes (an idea I was glad to have learned from others!). In time, the Lord allowed those classes to become a video course for children and families across the country. It has been exciting to pray that as the signs are learned, that the character of Christ, which parents are teaching, would also be reinforced as the children are watching!

The story still does not stop here. I received a call from a local college to interpret for two deaf students. Although the hours were short, it paid enough to supplement my income during some financially tight months for GraceWorks. That opportunity ended as one student graduated and the other transferred to a different school. Yet a few months later, I received a call from the college asking if I would be interested in teaching a sign language course for adults within their program. This seemed a shocking thought! How would I teach adults? What material would I use? Well, the only material I had was "Signs for His Glory" and so I swallowed hard, put my shoulders back and began using nearly the same material with this new class of students.

To make a long story short, the Lord has now allowed me to teach seven different classes and currently He has given nearly fifty students. Though the focus is more strongly on character than the Biblical background of it, the exciting potential for teaching character is that it lays the groundwork for presenting Christ. There is something within us that tells us that there is indeed right and wrong. If there is no God, then who placed this moral code upon our hearts? And how do we know what is good, what is acceptable? How can we understand or define love, for example, if God has not Himself demonstrated it to us? Otherwise, it is only my opinion, or yours, that defines love.

I was asked by some deaf friends to interpret for a Gospel presentation tomorrow night. I eagerly invited my classes to attend and was amazed at their response! Of course they are excited to watch someone interpreting, to see how many signs they can understand, but of course I am excited for a different reason!

Our class ends in two weeks and I made special scrolls with a beautiful poem about the grace of God, written by a deaf/blind man~ the most touching poem I have ever read. I tied these with wired ribbon and included a booklet showing the "bridge illustration," a clear way of explaining the Gospel. I plan to share as I give their "gift" that this message has changed my life forever. Only God himself could open such a door to this "captive audience" of nearly fifty adults each week. I pray each week as I go, realizing that this is a "mission field" that God has given at this time in my life.

But how did this all begin? As an attempt to do something "great?" No, just as an effort to reach out to one friend who seemed lonely. It seems God so often chooses to work this way. Not when *we* have planned it, but only as His grace empowers us to be faithful to Him in the "small" ways. Did I have great strength or skill in my own self? No, quite the contrary. Looking back I can see that only God could have orchestrated the events that brought me to this place. The whole process has taken fourteen years. Had I aimed that many years ago to teach college students and share the Gospel with them, I would have failed, trying to bring it about in my own strength and time. And what valuable lessons would I have missed along the way?! No, it is not in seeking the end goal, but in being faithful to what God is telling us to do today that His will is accomplished in and through us.

No One is Cheering!

But what if in seeking to follow the Lord people react against us? How do we respond? The first thing we must do is something we might not initially think of. We must check our own attitudes. Many times when people react negatively, it is because they sense that we have a wrong attitude or spirit. Possibly we are prideful or seem judgmental or insincere. If we realize this is the case, it is up to us to go back to them and make things right. We must ask God to purify our motives. May we do all unto Him alone, and have a heart full of His love toward the individuals we are serving.

If we sincerely believe that our attitudes are right however, and we have a pure heart of love toward others, then we must offer even our reputation to the Lord and continue boldly (yet humbly!) in the way that He has led. The fact that someone disagrees with us does not necessarily mean that we are wrong. Keep in mind that another person is never your enemy, but that the true enemy of our souls is forever seeking to divide and destroy.

Lasting Investments

Faithfulness now, dividends then... As appealing as marriage may seem, I have thought at times that I could struggle with this change in my lifestyle. I have been so active as a single person and have the freedom to do anything that my family and I have felt God calling me to do. As I look at marriage, it would mean a more normal, slower-paced life (at least for a while!) and although this might seem a welcome change at first, I can see some aspects that could be challenging. Becoming one in spirit means that the husband and wife become a ministry team, and for women, that means that we may need to give up many of our desires in order to support the goals and visions that God has given to our husbands. For example, if I married and my heart felt burdened to go to China, I could not pack my bags unless the Lord laid the same burden on the heart of my husband. This is a wonderful reason for us as single women to fight against an "independent spirit," something our world promotes as a valued quality. Right now our dependence and direction should be sought of those in direct authority over us, and ultimately from the Lord Himself. When we marry, the earthly side of that dependence is transferred to our husband.

What is the focus of one under authority? To please and make successful the one(s) we are serving. And we can take comfort that each one that is in authority over us is also under authority, to whom they are accountable. For no one except God Himself is a final authority. Yet our focus must be on how God (our ultimate authority) would have us respond to them, and trust the Lord to work in them the heart that He would want them to exemplify.

Many wives struggle to feel a sense of purpose amidst the vast number of "daily things" that consume their time. Their lives are full of taking care of their home and children~ vital and valuable tasks indeed, (and ones I look forward to someday, if the Lord allows!) yet often they feel isolated from outside ministry. Although some of this relates to the importance of having joyful and willing obedience within our circumstances, let me challenge us while we are single to make investments now that will continue to draw interest after we marry.

Allow me to share a simple story to help illustrate this. A dear friend, whom I had not seen for a long time, called about getting together for lunch. We can't remember a time we did not know each other. We played dolls as children and learned some hard lessons of life together as we grew up. Now we are older~ and God has blessed her with a real "doll" of her own. We planned a lunch together and I cannot tell you how eager I was to see this precious friend! At the same time, I was feeling great pressure within GraceWorks. When the day came for our lunch, the pressure continued. Just before leaving to meet my friend, I remembered a large number of pages that needed to be printed from our computer. Knowing these would take a couple of hours to complete, I loaded my printer and began the process just before I left. It seems like such a simple thing, but I cannot tell you how refreshing our lunch was to me, just knowing that work was being done, even in my absence! Even during this busy time, I was able to sit back and fully enjoy each moment with my precious friend, and focus all of my energies (without guilt!) on our time together.

Could it not be the same way, only to a greater degree when we are married? That we would invest now in things that would continue to bear fruit after we are married, and even into eternity? How exciting to have the opportunity to "focus on the Lord and what is well pleasing to Him" while we are single! Then, if the Lord would lead us to marriage, our hearts can be fully there, not wishing we could go back and have the opportunities to minister for the Lord as we could when we were single. We will still have great opportunities to minister, but they will be of a new nature, and the opportunities we once had will be forever gone. God only knows the number of years or months we have left to serve Him in this unparalleled way. Live each month as if it were your last to give! What a privilege it will be, and how humbled we will feel, as God someday allows us to lay these "treasures of singleness" at His feet, our offering of praise and gift of worship to Him!

Questions:

1) When as a child, my mother watched my grandfather plant a tree. Seeing her watching, he said You plant trees for your grandchildren." Those trees grew up sure enough, to the pleasure of my sister and I! What "trees" have you planted that could lend benefits to the future as you continue to nurture and allow them to grow?

2) What skills do you think would be important for you to begin developing right now?

3) Explain the way that you are building in these three areas: Gold, Silver, and Precious Stones.

4) Which of these areas is in greatest need of strengthening? What plan of action could you take?

5) How could you make a more focused effort toward becoming an effective prayer warrior?

6) Would you kneel right now and ask the Lord to place within your heart a burning desire to be more faithful in this discipline and devoted to Him in this way?

Additional Support:

• Verses: Isaiah 58:10,11; I Cor. 4:1,2; Psa. 1:3

• Tools: *"He Shall Hear My Voice"* a print by C. Michael Dudash The most beautiful, inspiring painting I have ever seen, capturing not only the spirit of prayer, but heart that this book seeks to share with us as women.

• Resources: *Answers to Prayer* (George Mueller) An inspiring glimpse into this man of prayer that will cause you to look at your own prayer life with more eagerness and resolve!

She girdeth her loins with strength,

& Strengtheneth her arms

*H*ollywood has tried to convince us that there is an outward physical ideal to be coveted, that there is a height of physical perfection to be attained. Yet the Bible says that we are "fearfully and wonderfully made" and that God created each of us according to His special design. Surely we are all quite different. Some are big-boned, some are small-boned, some are short, others are tall. No amount of exercise can change that structure. Some have troublesome skin, others seem to have a flawless complexion, some have perfectly refined features and hair that seems to "fall" into place when they crawl out of bed in the morning. *(I know, truly, life is not fair!)*. God has designed our bodies in amazing ways. and we must each accept the way that God lovingly made us. Yet God made us each unique for a purpose and as we accept the way that we are made and are able to thank Him for it, we are able to give ourselves back to Him in a special way.

Once we accept His gift, we can realize we do have a certain amount of influence over the temple God has given. When we think of needing to be in good physical shape, we must consider keeping our bodies in a condition that is both a good testimony for the Lord and in a way that gives us the strength to serve Him. At the same time we must be careful that in seeking to maintain ourselves in a way that would please Him, that we do not become over-occupied with ourselves, making comparisons with others. Our aim is not to "beautify" ourselves, but rather to have an outward appearance that testifies and radiates what the Lord has done in our hearts.

Being in good physical condition helps us in so many ways as well. It gives us more endurance and energy as we go about our day, it strengthens our immune system, it helps us sleep better at night, it even releases endorphins that contribute to a more positive, encouraged outlook on life. In my own life, I cannot tell you how much more stamina I have when I have even devoted a little time to exercise during the week. I almost feel like a different person when I am faithful in this discipline. Though at times, this seems impossible to fit in, I realize that it is more than just exercise— it is like taking an energy pill that energizes me to be more diligent and efficient at carrying out the work God gives me to do. This is to say nothing of the benefit continuous years of exercise may be later in life.

Healthy eating is also important. Often we do not reap the consequences of a poor diet for years to come. The American Cancer Society estimates that more than one-third of the 560,000 cancer deaths projected to occur in our country in the next year will be nutrition related, and therefore many could have been prevented. Most of our wrong choices lie in eating too many fats and sweets, and not enough fruits, vegetables and whole grains (my finger points back at me as I write!). Eating healthy is a battle for many, especially those of us who often eat on our own. It is hard to convince ourselves to take the time to prepare food for "just for one," especially when there are so many things that busy our lives.

Reading about nutrition and what chemicals and fats do to our bodies, as well as what our body does with the good things that we feed it, has been a great help to me. Not only has it given me an understanding of why nutrition is so vitally important, it has helped me to begin changing some of my habits as well. For example, did you know that the majority of calcium our body will store, will be put away before we turn thirty? After that point, we are able to do little more than to keep from losing that which we have. Did you know the body is made up of between 50% to 70% water? For years I was not getting enough of this "liquid of life" and began suffering for it.

If you are not exercising at all right now, think of how you might include even twenty minutes, two or three times a week. Of course, the ideal is higher, but this is a great place to begin. If you eat poorly, try to add two fruits or vegetables each day, and work toward including five. Drink more water. Take Selenium, Vitamin E, Calcium, and Vitamin C. These, along with a multi-vitamin, will help keep your body, God's temple, in good condition.

Do not be deceived!

I feel compelled to add a note of caution. Just as in any other area, satan always wants to get us out of balance. He will try to get our attention over-focused on our bodies, our eating, or our exercise. When we begin to reject the way God made us, we become susceptible to lies satan brings. Bulimia and anorexia are two of these. We are fooled as we allow our thoughts to be consumed with how we look and begin to believe that the way that God made us is not good enough. We find ourselves seeking the approval of others above the approval of God. Once a damaging eating habit is started, it is difficult to quit. If satan is trying to deceive you in this area, realize his deception and stubbornly refuse to accept it as truth. Never underestimate the use of God's Word as your defense. Memorize Psalm 139, and absorb yourself in thoughts of the Lord and your time in serving others. This is a double blessing in that it forces you to focus on others, and they are blessed in the process! If you have already found yourself involved in this dangerous cycle, don't keep it a secret from those that love you. Satan would have you keep it hidden, but for your own good, reach out to get the help that you need.

Inner Strength

We could have perfect physical health, yet if we neglect the health of our spirit, we can never be ready to make a difference for Christ, nor experience the richness in fellowship that He wants us to share. Just as we need physical nutrients to survive, our soul needs "fresh air" from above and "water" from the Living springs to be strong and healthy spiritually.

Soldiers go to battle armed and ready for war. And the Bible reminds us repeatedly that we are in a war as well. So how do we become effective in the midst of the battle that we are facing? First of all, we must consider how well we know the Word of God, the "Sword of the Spirit," and how capable are we in using it effectively. Possibly we can get through some Bible stories with few flaws, but do we really know the Bible? Do we really know what it says? Are we seeking to understand its doctrines that we might "be ready always" to give an answer, and detect false teaching as it comes our way?

In writing about cults, David Breese shares that the fundamental reason we as Christians are deceived by false teaching is because we do not know the Word of God. Followers of false religions spend hours pouring over their own religious books, seeking how they might convince others to believe their doctrines. Yet God says:

"My people are destroyed for lack of knowledge " (Hosea 4:6)

Our quest for this knowledge may have been daunted by our culture's attempt to do away with God. Yet this is why it is all the more important that we have a solid, unshakable belief in the reliability of God's Word. Often those of us who have grown up in Christian families to believe the Bible only because it is what we have been taught from birth. We never really develop a foundation in our own hearts that we can skillfully defend. Josh McDowell wrote an insightful book, *"Evidence That demands a verdict, Historical Evidences for the Christian Faith."* Here he says:

> *"Christianity it either EVERYTHING for mankind, or NOTHING. It is either the highest certainty or the greatest delusion... But if Christianity be EVERYTHING for mankind, it is important for every man to be able to give a good reason for the hope that is in him in regard to the eternal verities of the Christian faith. To accept these verities in an unthinking way, or to receive them simply on authority, is not enough for an intelligent and stable faith."*

Apologist Clark Pinnock writes:

> *"An intelligent Christian ought to be able to point up the flaws in a non-Christian position and to present facts and arguments which tell in favor of the gospel. If our apologetic prevents us from explaining the gospel to any person, it is an inadequate apologetic."*

At a recent conference, the speaker challenged "Do you believe the Bible is truth because *you* believe it, or do you believe the Bible because *it is truth?*" In our society, truth has come to mean "whatever I personally believe to be true" instead of being defined as absolute truth (meaning something that is always true in all circumstances, with all people). If satan causes you to doubt, or if you are hesitant to "speak truth" because you are afraid of questions arising which you cannot answer, this is a spiritual muscle that can be strengthened!

If we want to be effective in sharing the Gospel with others, it is crucial that we have a solid understanding of it ourselves. Although the Lord has worked through the mouths of children in turning lost souls to Him, we will become better equipped to share as we learn more of Him and less likely to unintentionally mislead. I have appreciated the challenge of Ray Comfort in his video "The Ten Cannons." He shares that when we witness by telling another that their life will become happier and more wonderful if they become saved~ not only do we give them a wrong motive for being saved, we set them up for failure when they later find that life is still hard and full of sorrows. The Bible calls the law of God a "schoolmaster" (Gal. 3:24), leading a sinner to repentance. We need to lovingly take them to the Scriptures and help them to see that God's law cannot be broken without consequence. And that they, just like we, have a desperate need for Christ's forgiveness of sin and eternal salvation from death and hell. Though we could never come to a place of being all knowledgeable, the more we do know of God and His Word, the more we have from which to draw. While you should never let a lack of knowledge keep you from sharing, you will be blessed as you seek to strengthen this vital area!

Prepared to Deceive

Once I was looking at Internet sites related to planners. I stumbled across a planning system a prominent cult has created for themselves. They have pages for keeping track of witnessing, prayers for those who are outside of their beliefs, a page for keeping track of their own "spiritual" disciplines, and even a "redeeming the dead page" *(I know, that one was frightful for me to consider as well!~ they believe that their prayers and works can have an effect on the eternal destinies of those who have "gone before.")*. Though I could not agree with their doctrine, I certainly had to admire their diligence and fervor. About this same time I had been working on some new ministry pages for GraceWorks. I had felt discouraged as to the importance of their completion. "Will people really use these?" I wondered. "Will *I* use them?" Yet my resolve to have them printed was strengthened as I saw this web page. Why do we as Christians so rarely consider the task laid before us? Why don't we have a *plan* for ministry to the lost? If we *know* the Truth, why don't we have a passion to share it with others? Why do we allow ourselves to be so easily distracted by the transitory things of life, and spend so little time in preparation for ministry? Will you, with me, purpose to be more deeply devoted to His higher calling, and furthermore, make it a planned, thought-out way of life?

One Vital Tool

Certainly, reading Christian books can help us understand how to better evangelize and how to separate truth from lie, yet the most effective tool we have been given is the holy Word of God. There is one discipline most crucial to your health as a Christian, which doubles as an encourager in your desire to glorify God. I'm speaking of memorizing, and then meditating on, the Word of God.

We have come to a time in our society when we rarely memorize anything. Where memorization of poetry and facts used to be considered a noble and respected task, today with so much material readily available and the "dumbing down" of our society, memorization has become a lost art.

It was once said: *"God gave us memory, so that we might have roses in December."* Such a beautiful thought, and not only roses in the coldest of our earthly seasons, but also that we might have "roses" in the winters of the soul~ the comforts and promises of God's Word.

Hidden in Our Hearts

One can never know the rich blessings of memorizing Scripture until it she experiences it personally. I grew up memorizing Scripture, so possibly it has a special place in my heart for that reason. Nevertheless, it has always been hard work. I have had the conviction of my need for it, the desire to follow through, and even the actual doing of it, yet I have always had to work hard at it. It seemed that few Scriptures really "stuck," even those I had tried repeatedly to memorize. Certainly there is no harm in working on a verse again and again. It often reveals fresh insights. And as N.A. Woychuk points out "we must not allow ourselves to think that *all* of the verses memorized are forgotten. This is simply not true. We never quite forget all that we have diligently memorized." This thought is a great comfort, yet I saw the need more accurately remember the Word of God, that I might first of all, know Him better, that I might live out His Word moment by moment, and use it in encouraging Christians and pro-claiming truth to those who are lost in confusion and falsehood.

Because I lack for space here, I will wait for the second book to share this plan that has worked wonderfully for me. I will just say that whereas before I would struggle to learn even a verse or two in a week, over the last months, the Lord has allowed me to learn six, sometimes twelve in a week. I do not say that to my honor! I say it because for years I tried to be faithful in this discipline, and met so often with defeat. I would be more than happy to even send you an explanation of it if that would be helpful to you.

A Vital Key for Life-Changing Memorization

As I attended a recent convention, a man taught on three different types of prayer. The first is the prayer of our *mouth,* this can be seen as rote, memorized prayers~ "Now I lay me down to sleep..."; the sec-ond was prayer of the *mind* ~ that we say in order to impress someone with our intellect or spirituality; and the third was a prayer of the *heart,* when we cry out to God, having come to the end of ourselves. Psalms 51:17 says *"The sacrifices of God are a broken spirit, a broken and contrite heart, O God, Thou wilt not despise."* He sees our humility, and that realization of our need is precious to Him. Think of the story of the Pharisee and the Publican. The Pharisee prayed piously "Lord, I thank you that I am not a sinner like he." whereas the Publican could not even look up to heaven as he cried out to the Lord for mercy. I so appreciated this powerful teaching and as I thought about it later, I realized that it is also descriptive of the ways that we memorize Scripture.

Memorizing with our lips: In visiting with an old school friend, she remarked that when she was young, she could take her memory book, look at it for a few minutes, walk out into the hall and recite it perfectly for the "hearer." She fulfilled her "duty," but how did she memorize? From her lips. She was able to speak it that day, but would have likely been hard-pressed to say it the very next.

*M*emorizing with our minds: It has been a joy to challenge children to be diligent in this discipline, and I am amazed at their diligence in learning (and thus challenged myself!). Yet as I hear them recite their verses, I don't know if they are memorizing it deep enough for it to have the full impact that it could be having on their young hearts and lives. They truly remember their verses~ one can say an entire memory booklet in a breath and a half (more than thirty verses!). Yet although their diligence is commendable (and far beyond most adults!) it seems that at this point most of their memorization stays within their minds. I don't know that their motive is to impress me, so much as it is to *please* me (which is an endearing motive, indeed), yet I think that I have dropped the ball of responsibility in not realizing the need to challenge them beyond the memorizing of the words. Last year I was at a camp and asked one young camper if he could recite a verse. After he did so quite well, I continued by asking him, "What does that mean?" Without hesitation he shrugged and said "I don't know!" and ran away!

*M*emorizing with our hearts: If we want to memorize in a way that will strengthen us in the Lord and bless others, we must not only be able to speak the verses on our lips, or remember them in our minds, we must also allow them to seep deep into our hearts! Possibly the key to this comes in the powerful step that comes right after memorization. We will talk about this in a few moments!

Purpose in Memorizing

Say someone came to your door selling "gidgets," you would wisely be hesitant to buy one unless you were convinced you had a need. But then, once you were truly convinced, and if you realized that your need for this item was critical, you would be willing to pay nearly any cost to have a gidget of your very own. In the same way, if you do not see a need to memorize Scripture, you will not be willing to make the sacrifices necessary to be effective in this discipline. Certainly, as we have already discussed, it is God's will and desire that we engraft His

Word into our hearts. So our first reason should be out of pure obedience to Him. Yet there are many other reasons as well. Though it would be impossible to list all of these benefits, here are a few that have been the most significant in my life:

1) Changing Me Recently I was in a situation where my patience was being extremely tried. I began to be upset and was feeling an urge rise within me to react. Without conscious thought, the words *"the patience of Christ"* from II Thessalonians 3:5 rang through my mind. I had not been praying for grace, nor had I thought of much... other than how terribly I wanted to react. Yet there were those sweet words, invading some pretty frustrated territory. And you know, immediately my heart was softened. I thought, even as I continued in that situation, *"What is the "patience of Christ?' The patience of Christ is being spat upon, being mocked, being ridiculed, being beaten, being nailed upon a wicked tree with nails of hate, and enduring it all, not reviling because of love for His persecutors."* As I considered this attribute of Christ I thought, *"No, I have not been asked to show such a degree of patience. Not ever."* And thus my heart was changed, my tongue bridled and my thoughts sweetened and convicted.

Had I not memorized that verse, would it have been brought to mind at that time? No. Did I request it to come when it did? No again. The Holy Spirit clearly brought it as He promised He would (John 25:25-26). Because God had allowed me to memorize and meditate upon this verse in the past, it was an available weapon to be used on my behalf when the enemy came. So often we try to change ourselves by creating rules or just "deciding" we are going to be different. And while these may work for a time, it is only the Word of God that will bring lasting change to our lives, only His Word that "returneth not void."

2) Ministry to Others Have you ever been in a situation where you knew you had memorized a verse that was desperately "needed" for the moment but simply could not recall it? I cannot count the times I've been there myself. The Bible exhorts us to be ready *"in sea-*

son and out of season..." (II Tim. 4:2) ~ prepared, not just with our own futile words, but the living words of God. By regular review of your verses, you will be greatly helped in this area. Yet I am excited to share in the second book a way of memorizing that will soundly secure verses in your mind in a way that makes immediate recall of them in these situations nearly flawless!

3) Enhancement of Scripture Study Another benefit is realized as we read other areas of the Bible. Every verse that you memorize will bring insight and add depth to new passages you read. Bible reading becomes exciting as your mind learns to compare what you are reading with the verses you have engrafted in your heart. Without realizing it, you will find yourself pulling verses and sections of verses out of memory as you read other passages. This not only helps you to better understand what you read, but to understand the complete truth of God's Word.

4) Promised Success The Bible promises great blessing as we memorize and meditate upon His Word, for only then can our hearts and desires be in line with His. Joshua 1:8 says: *"This book of the law shall not depart out of thy mouth; but thou shalt meditate therein day and night, that thou mayest observe to do according to all that is written therein: for then thou shalt make thy way prosperous, and then thou shalt have good success."* As our hearts are molded after His, then He changes our desires to be like His. We must remember that we must allow God to define success~ I can imagine that Moses felt very unsuccessful after walking away from Pharaoh that *ninth* time, yet it was all in God's plan~ and little did he know that God would turn Pharaoh's heart the very next time!

Meditation, an Exciting Key!

We are told in Joshua to "meditate day and night," but that may seem a little nebulous. A friend of our family's, who is all of five years old, was asked by his mother to turn off a flashlight he was using under his covers, it was time for him to go to sleep. When he peeked out, the source of his concentration was revealed~ his "Scripture book."

He looked at his mother questionably and asked sincerely, *"But Mother, how am I suppose to meditate day and night?"* We smile at his precious answer, but what an amazing depth it reveals in the heart of this young boy!

But what *does* it *really* mean to meditate? The world has tried to reap the benefits of meditating as well, but their method is completely different than God's. The world's way is to empty ones mind of all thought. But to leave a mind empty, places it in serious danger of being filled with destructive things. God's way of meditation is just the opposite, that we might *fill* our minds with *His* thoughts and *His* ways. After you have memorized a verse, ask God to work it into your heart. Think of what God meant as He inspired it, what application it can have to your life today, what things in your life need to be changed in order for it to be lived out, and how it can be used to bless and exhort others. Take that verse and emphasize different words and consider the meaning of each aspect. Meditation is taking time to focus our minds on Scripture, that our thoughts might be "stayed on Him" throughout the day. It is thinking God's thoughts with the intention of making them ours, aligning our hearts with His.

George Mueller, known primarily as a man of prayer, realized at one point in his ministry that although beginning each day in prayer was beneficial, it was by far *more* fruitful to...

> *"meditate on the Word of God, searching as it were into every verse to get the blessing out of it... in order to obtain food for my own soul... so that, though I did as it were, give myself to prayer, but to meditation, yet it turned almost immediately more or less into prayer... Food for my soul is the object of my meditation. The result is that there is always a good deal of confession, thanksgiving, supplication, or intercession mingled with my meditation."*

Increasing Your Mental Abilities

Countless testimonies have been given by those that have struggled in school, that the simple habit of memorizing and meditating on

Scripture has significantly increased their mental abilities. I think that this is the result of both the Lord blessing the individual's faithfulness in this area, and the benefit that this type of "exercise" is to the mind.

Amazing research has been done, demonstrating that listening to Baroque music as you learn (such as Bach, Beethoven & Handel), allows you to process information at a much faster pace. Furthermore, your retention is much greater, even weeks later. I have tried this and have been surprised at how it has helped me thus far. Probably most significant for me is the recall that it allowed me to have at later times, as I had very specific, word for word recall~ even weeks later (as at one time I was certain that I could scarcely learn facts or verses "for keeps!"). You try it and I would love to hear what you find!

Keeping Sight of the Goal

There is no "right way" or "perfect number" of verses to memorize. In fact, if we learned thousands and as a result became prideful in our knowledge, all would be lost. The goal is not to see how many verses we can learn or quote, but rather that we might deepen our knowledge of Him so that in knowing Him, our ways might become more like His. I can say honestly for myself, that my growth and maturity as a Christian has always seemed to parallel my faithfulness and obedience in this area.

Questions:

1) Are you being certain to give your body all the nutrients that it needs to be healthy for the Lord? Are there any changes you should make?

2) Do you have a deep enough understanding of your faith that you could adequately explain it to someone that asked you specific questions about how you believe?

3) Certainly there are questions that we will be asked that we will need to study in order to answer, but how are you actively seeking to strengthen that foundation so that you are better prepared to "be ready always to give a reason?"

4) Are you actively memorizing Scripture?

5) Have you ever truly meditated on a verse of Scripture? Are you doing this now?

6) How can you plan to implement/continue in this discipline?

7) Who will hold you accountable?

Additional Support:

- Verses: I Cor. 6:19-20; Josh. 1:8; II Tim. 2:24-26; 3:16,17; Isa. 50:4, Col.3:16

- Tools: *Music and the Mind* (Audio Cassette) ~ a fascinating explanation of the effect music has on learning and the mind

- Resources: Evidence that Demands a Verdict (Josh McDowell), *You Need to Memorize Scripture* (N.A. Woychuk)

Choose a special verse to commit to memory and write it below:

She perceiveth that her merchandise is good: her candle goeth not out by night.

*D*aniel asked the king if he and his men could be put on a special diet that they knew was pleasing to the Lord. After being on their diet for ten days, the king was to evaluate them to see if they were not stronger and healthier than the other men of the kingdom. And what happened? They were found to be exceedingly outstanding! In the same way, the quality of our lives and work should be outstanding as it reflects the character Christ is building in our hearts!

It has often been said that if something is worth doing, it is worth doing well. Although one might find exceptions to this rule, there is certainly a good reason for maintaining a standard of excellence in one's life. This does not mean perfection, rather aiming to excel as you seek to please the Lord. In doing this, you also allow others to praise Him when they see the godly seed you are sowing!

"Let your light so shine before men, that they may see your good works and glorify you Father which is in heaven." Mt. 5:16

Is there a radiance about your face, a sparkle in your step, an "extra touch" in what you do? What about your work? If someone asks you to complete a job, will it be completed fully and in a way that shows care and thought?

Becoming a Mystery

"Whatever thy hand findeth to do," we are told in Ecclesiastes 9:10, *"do it with thy might."* In Psalms, it tells repeatedly that we are to serve the Lord with a *whole* heart. Most people in the world are content in seeking to meet their own needs and to fulfill only the bare minimum expected of them. We should be the opposite~ serving in such a way that people realize we are different~ that like Daniel, we become a token of God's grace and power at work in our lives. Though people might not initially be interested in the God we serve, as they wonder at the fruit of His character in our lives, God may be using this to their hearts toward Him!   turn

The Bible tells us of people who were a bad testimony for the Lord. In () it tells us that the non-Christians laughed at God because of the behavior of His people. This is one reason God gives such strong commands against being lukewarm. If we claim His holy Name, yet live no differently than those who do not, then not only will we give them reason to mock, but we will also take away their reason for hope. Are you a mystery to those God has placed around you? Would unsaved acquaintances say *"Well, I sure don't believe in God, but I must admit she's got something different."* Seek to become a "mystery," while never allowing that mystery to remain unsolved, allow it to open doors of ministry and then pray for God to bring opportunities for sharing the reason for that hope that lies within!

Preparation- an Important Key

The second half of our chapter verse *("her candle goeth not out by night")* may give some cause for concern. When one compares this verse with *"she riseth also while it is yet night"* it may seem at first that our dear Yaqar never slept! Yet we know that she did, for she dealt with the same human limitations as we. It is my understanding that in saying her candle did not go out at night, the implication was not that she did not sleep, rather that her candle kept burning as she slept. Remember the parable of the ten virgins? Some were able to leave when the bridegroom came, and the others were not. Why? Because not all of them were prepared. In the same way, we see that Yaqar lived prepared. In her day, people were dependent on fire for many of their most basic needs~ for light, cooking and warmth. If the flame in their homes went out, a great resource was lost until it was lit again. To say that "her candle did not go out" meant that she was prepared with all she needed to keep that light burning. She carefully secured all she needed ahead of time, in order to keep her home running smoothly.

Once I was listening to an interview with Donna Otto, a very dear Christian author and speaker. She spoke of the importance of being prepared. "If I have a meeting to attend tomorrow night, I should think 'What do I need to do in order to be prepared to go?'" When I first heard this principle, it almost seemed too simple to work. Yet I tried it and I was amazed! As one who has struggled with arriving on time to anything, this has been a great help to me~ and possibly it will be a great help to you as well. One of my greatest challenges is that I tend to try to fit too many things into my day and often don't allow myself the time needed to get ready for a new activity and gather my things to leave. Other times I may be fully ready to go out the door, when suddenly I will remember something that I need to take with me. Either I can't find the item, or it takes longer than I imagined to gather or wrap, and I realize with great discouragement that once again, I will be late! I began enacting this "preparedness principle" just after I heard it, and what a difference it has made! I have begun to establish the habit of gathering all I need for a given event several hours before it is time to leave. I have a place by the door where I can keep these items, and there they sit, waiting obediently for me as I leave the house! How this little principle has simplified my life!

Prepared to Encourage

We can also live prepared in many other areas of life. I remember that my grandmother would always have homemade cookies in the freezer, ready to pull out hospitably, as unexpected guests came or to take to a family in need of loving encouragement. They were always a welcome treat to her grandchildren, I can say from personal experience! Are you minister others, even unexpectedly?

Are you faithful in writing thank-you notes and letters of encouragement? Even short letters can mean so much! Create for yourself a small "writing center." This can be either a desk or a simple shoe box. In this place, keep stationary, envelopes, addresses and a book of stamps. After receiving a gift or letter, quickly write their name and address on an envelope and place a stamp on it. You will feel like your work is half done! Then in the next few days, find a moment to write the letter or thank-you note. I was once convicted to hear: "It is far better to be *ungrateful* than to be *grateful* and neglect to show it."

To keep track of birthdays, make a list on a piece of paper and keep it in a prominent place. Taping it to the top-inside of your box may be the most logical spot, and if you use that box faithfully, you will never miss another birthday again!

Lessons in Letter-Writing

As we write, we should consider what we can do to make our letters the greatest encouragement. This does not mean that our letters need to be long, but written with genuine concern. In one of her books, Elisabeth Elliot told of some of the letters she received on the mission field. Here are two examples similar to those that she received, notice the vast difference between them.

Dear Elisabeth,

Hope you are well. Here is a check from the board. Things here are about the same. We are voting next Tuesday on whether we will rearrange the order of the Sunday morning service or not..."

Dear Elisabeth,

Hello, how I pray you are well! So often I wonder how you are and what you are doing. Please tell me about your surroundings, as I struggle to picture you there and all you are doing. How do you spend your time? What are the people like? What are the burdens of your heart? How can we be praying for you?"

Such a difference! Letter-writing becomes a truly worthwhile task as we seek to encourage and exhort the one we are addressing. This is good to consider for any letter we might write. If it be a thank you note, don't just say "Thank you for the stationary." But complement on the design and how you will use it. Always show gratefulness for their generosity and praise qualities that you see in their life. Even if you receive a gift that you do not like, you can still send a very warm, gracious note. You might say "Thank you so much for the shirt which you gave me for my birthday..." ("It is such a beautiful color, or very comfortable," or anything that you might honestly be able to say about it!) "You have been so thoughtful and it always warms my heart to realize the love and concern you continually show to me."

A Late Night Distress Call

After driving a few hours to pick up students from a missions trip, we suddenly developed significant car problems as we left the airport. It was late at night and there was no hope of repair until morning. We ended up imposing on a dear family in the area~ all twenty of us descended upon their house as they generously pulled together as many blankets and beds as they could muster! Upon arriving back home, a card of gratefulness was circulated to be sent in response to their kindness to us. Yet what a disappointment when I set out to mail it, that not *one single note* contained anything beyond "thanks for letting us stay at your house." We had invaded their home very late at night, rearranged their entire schedule for several hours, and all we could say was "thanks for letting us stay at your house?"

I don't believe that any one of them were intending to be ungrateful, yet it would have been so easy to write in a way that would have truly blessed its recipients. Expressing sincere gratefulness takes so little time~ one could say: "I cannot tell you how we appreciated your kindness to us. We were all so tired and weary, yet what a welcome relief to have such a comfortable place to stay..." or "We cannot thank you enough for the incredible hospitality you showed to our group last week. God used you to minister not only to our physical needs, but also to bless us with the kindness of your friendship..."

A Prepared Heart

"Ezra prepared his heart to seek the law of the LORD,
and to do it, and to teach..." Ezra 7:10

Before going to church or a Bible Study, don't simply get ready *physically*, spend time with the Lord, preparing *spiritually*. Many times we miss out on rich lessons and blessings the Lord wants to give because our minds are consumed with other things, and not with Him.

"How many times have you... spent more time about decorating your body to go to Church, than you have about preparing your mind for the worship of God? You have gone caring more as to how you appeared outwardly in the sight of mortal man, than how your soul appeared in the sight of the heart-searching God." Charles Finney

In the same way, we should daily ask the Lord to make ready our hearts to minister to others. It is so easy in a group setting to focus on ourselves~ our own promotion and enjoyment, and miss out on God's plan for us to be a comfort and blessing to others! As we spend time meditating upon His Word and ways we might edify others, we will be significantly strengthened and brought into a frame of mind that is well prepared for God to use in ministry.

Discouragement

But what if you serve very diligently, in great hopes of opening wide doors of ministry to others but no one ever seems to notice your efforts or express even small amounts of gratefulness for your investment in them? You've read the verse from Matthew that tells of people noticing good works and glorifying our Heavenly Father, but you feel your efforts are not having this effect. This happens in the workplace, in the home, and even in ministry environments. And although you may not set out to work with the intent of inspiring praise from those around you, it is certainly something that the human heart desires. We want to know we are pleasing to those around us, that our efforts are making a difference, that what we are doing really does matter.

Yet there are going to be times in our lives that we are going to be under an employer, or a leader that will never pat us on the back and say "job well done." Maybe at times this person will even be a parent. What do we do when we feel like we are unable to ever please one that we respect and admire, one that we have done everything within our power to please? Well, first of all in any situation where we struggle with the way one acts, we must consider that something has happened or failed to happen in that persons background that has caused them to be "handicapped" in their ability to respond properly. Possibly they came from a family that never gave them praise, and thus they never learned how to share it with others. Or maybe there were some hurts in their life that they have never fully dealt with. Often when others do not respond to us in a positive way, it is only a symptom of hurt that is yet below the surface. If we ask the Lord for hearts of love toward them and begin to pray for God to bring them joy and healing in any areas that may be yet untreated, God will begin a greater work in our own hearts of love and affection toward them.

In the meantime we must remember who we are really serving. Paul exhorted the slaves in the New Testament by saying "Servants, obey in all things your masters... not with eyeservice, as menpleasers; but in singleness of heart, fearing God." Can you imagine how it felt to be a slave? To work long hours, often in the hot sun, being beaten when your owner felt you weren't working quite up to par? There was no anticipation of any praise that these slaves would ever receive, yet Paul reminded them that it was the Lord that they were serving. Learn to expect that you won't be praised, and place all your expectation in the Lord. Know that someday He will say those beautiful words to you "Well done, thou good and faithful servant..." Glory in pleasing Him alone, even if no one else takes notice *("thy Father, which seeth in secret, shall reward thee..." Matt. 6:18).*

The "L" Word

We are reaching an exciting time in the book! Not so much because of anything that the book contains, but rather because of the vision I pray God is placing upon your own heart. And as you apply these principles (and those that God teaches you from other directions), I might ought to warn you that sooner or later, you are going to be joyfully serving your king, when out of the blue someone asks: "Aren't you getting a little legalistic?" In most cases this is a misguided question, yet it may break your heart to hear this from someone you love or respect. Let's consider it here for a moment so that we might be prepared with a beautiful, loving response.

First of all, as you have noticed in this book, we have often used athletes and competitions as comparatives. It is a most logical example, as there are many parallels in the goals, lives and high ideas of an athlete, and ours. So in this case, what if an olympian used this same rationale of not wanting to be "legalistic?" "I'm not going to train everyday~ why that would be legalistic. I will come in when I feel like it, when I feel inspired..." Or what if she refused to do her stretches each morning before attempting moves that placed great demands upon her muscles? What if she said "Coach, I don't think that your opinion of me should be based on my performance, or whether or not I follow your schedule, or aim to meet your requirements." And while her coach may indeed still care about her, he knows that with that attitude she will never win the gold.

And what is our goal as Christians in aiming high? First of all, it is a beautiful privilege we are given as Christians to serve within the kingdom! In Romans 8 it says that those of this world are slaves to darkness, but that we have been bought with a price, we belong to a new kingdom. Imagine if you were hired to serve an earthly king who was greatly admired and respected. Would we not feel privileged to have the honor of such service? It would be a great privilege indeed! Would we be embarrassed to take on the "royal garments" of the kingdom? Certainly not! In a similar way we have been given a high calling in serving our King, and are given "His garments" to wear. As our faces and lives reflect Him, we become vessels that He can use to draw others into His kingdom. And finally, and most important of all, our purpose is that we might please the One that gave His all for us. If I seek to please one that I love here on earth, I do not enjoy considering how much I can get away with and still maintain favor~ No! Rather I find *joy* in discovering what brings joy to that beloved's heart.

No one would call a husband "legalistic" for sending roses to his wife, or a wife for spending time to lovingly prepare dinner, night after night, for her husband. On the contrary, these are beautiful actions of love they willingly and gladly give to one another!

In the same way, there is great joy to be found in learning to please the Lord~ and no pleasure at all in seeing how much we can get away with, or how far His grace will reach. Romans 6:1 says "What shall we say then? Shall we continue in sin that grace may abound? God forbid!" The gift of grace is a beautiful one indeed, one without which none of us would cross through the gates of heaven. But it is a gift that God has lovingly given, not a cheap toy to be added to our toybox. If we truly desire to live for the Lord, then it will be our most natural response to turn our hearts toward the things that please Him. Josh Harris stated this principle so excellently when he said:

> "We cannot simultaneously explore the boundaries of purity and pursue righteousness—they point us in opposite directions."

Truly, if our hearts are directed toward God and seeking to please Him in all our ways, our desire to "test the limits" will begin to dissipate. The mindset of trying to find a "line" of sin will be of little concern because if you consider Josh's statement, our back will be to that line. We will be walking steadfastly toward righteousness, decidedly away from anything that is not pleasing to Him!

Help from Webster

For a definition of legalism, I opened a Webster's dictionary which defined it as "excessive conformity to a law or religious code; the doctrine of salvation by good works." It must be clear in our minds that there is nothing that we can do to earn salvation. As Ephesians 2:8,9 says: *"For by grace are ye saved through faith; and that not of yourselves: it is the gift of God: not of works, lest any man should boast."* We must realize our salvation is a separate issue than works, for as we just read, we are saved by *grace alone.* Yet at the same time, James connected them for us in this way: *"someone will say, 'You have faith, and I have works.' Show me your faith without your works, and I will show you my faith by my works."* He was simply saying that although our works do not bring salvation, they are certainly the fruits and proof of His sanctification at work in our lives.

Legalism is:

1) Believing our good works will get us to heaven.
2) Becoming so focused on doing right things that we lose sight of Him.
3) Forgetting we are saved by grace alone, and somehow hoping to atone for ourselves by works.
4) Having a prideful, holier-than-thou attitude to those who live differently.
5) Failing to express genuine love to others because of differing convictions

But Legalism is not:

1) Having a heart's desire to please God.
2) Turning from sin.
3) Choosing to live a radiant life for the Lord.
4) Making wise choices in deference to our brothers and sisters in Christ.
5) Choosing a way that is different from the world.
6) Realizing there *are* moral absolutes, some actions please God, others do not.
7) Attempting to live in joyful obedience to His Word.

It is important that we separate our *convictions* from our *preferences*. Convictions are areas placed in cement. We are commanded never to use the Lord's Name in vain. This never changes in any situation. On the other hand, preferences are decisions that we make in order to more greatly reflect the Lord and bless others. With these we may occasionally need to defer to a higher command.

One becomes legalistic when she becomes so focused on the law that she loses sight of its purpose and of the God she was initially seeking to serve. The following example might help in clarifying this point. Although I cannot say that legalism was truly in the heart of this young man, of whom I am about to share, certainly his actions at times came across in that way. His parents had once shared with him that they preferred he never be alone with a women in a car. Everyone that knew him fully respected his desire to uphold his parents wishes in this way. But one time on a ministry excursion, three of us were in a car when we stopped for gas. It tickled me, when as the other ventured to the pump, he dutifully stepped outside to stand beside his door until the tank was full.

Another time, I was walking home from work when it started pouring rain. I mean pouring! I was half way home and had no option other than to keep on walking. Then suddenly, I recognized his car coming down the street toward me. "Oh!" I thought with relief, "I'm going to be rescued!" Yet much to my disappointment he drove right on by without stopping (being a gentleman though, he did wave!). I was shocked~ and quite cold and wet by the time I reached home!

His character was impeccable~ I say this to his honor! Yet as I considered this issue, it seemed his high character should have brought him greater freedom to be able to defer to a sincere need. For example, had he given me a ride the day I got caught in the rain, if anyone would have observed his offer of a ride (even knowing his usual demeanor in this area), they would have only thought him to have had the noblest of intentions. It seemed that he was obeying the "letter of the law," instead of seeking to understand the spirit therein. The result of this kind of focus is that instead of turning attention to *the glory of God* for a life that pleases Him and blesses others, most often it becomes difficult not to place the attention on the *individual* or be *distracted* by the stringent adherence to the "law."

In all honesty though, I have met very few people that I suspected were actually legalistic. Though I know that there are individuals that might certainly fit in this category, I think more often than not, it is a term that we like to use to make us comfortable continuing in our own ways. We don't like the feeling of conviction and would rather find excuses than wholeheartedly seek what He wants for our lives.

Certainly there are hypocrites, those that try to do all the right things on the outside, possibly to alleviate guilt that they feel or in hopes that others will consider them "spiritual." The Bible speaks of this in Isaiah 29:13 *"Inasmuch as these people draw near to Me with their mouths and honor Me with their lips, But have removed their hearts far from Me..."* The Pharisees were legalists. They were so focused on rules (most of them

I Timothy

man-made requirements) that they could not even recognize the Son of God when He stood in their presence. Just as the church of Ephesus had lost their first love, so had the Pharisees. They had no true, loving relationship with the living God! Yet God desires that we turn our ways to be pleasing to Him. Too often as Christians we want to be saints without sacrifice, to be redeemed without repentance, to be saved without sanctification. Jesus Himself said in John 15:14, *"You are my friends if you do whatsoever I command."*

If you find yourself being asked this question, and truly believe that you are innocent of the charge, prayerfully respond with a loving, humble attitude. Smile and convey that you are convinced that your good deeds could never get you to heaven and just as pleasing someone you love on earth brings your heart joy, similarly you have found joy in considering how you might please and glorify the Lord!

Questions:

1) Is your life a mystery? Does it cause others to want to know the secret of your hope?

2) Are you prepared spiritually, physically and mentally for life?

3) In what ways do you need to become more prepared?

4) What is your plan for doing so?

5) Is there an area discussed in this chapter in which you realize you need to grow or change? What is it? What is your plan of action?

Additional Support:

• Verses: Num. 6:24-26; Phil. 2:12-16; Phil. 3:12-14; Rom. 16:19; Rom. 12:1,2; 12:10-15

• Tools: Italic Handwriting Books~ these help you to develop a more beautiful, legible "hand."

She layeth her hands to the spindle, & her hands hold the distaff.

Women are climbing the corporate ladders. There are more women in the work force now then there ever have been. Yet are women as a whole any happier than before? They certainly don't seem to be. Children and families are falling apart. As a nation we are none the happier, none the wiser. There was a special report done a few years ago by ABC's Nightline, about the direction our country has taken. It was aired just after there was a huge jump in our Gross Domestic Product (the amount of money being spent by our country as a whole). The assumption has been that the more people are spending, the more they are enjoying the life they pay so much to live. Yet they offered a different view. They looked back to the days of 'Leave it to Beaver' and 'Father Knows Best.' In these shows, the mother stayed home and took care of the house and children. She had a genuine, joyful understanding of her role, and a sincere respect for her husband who worked to provide for the family. This picture is quite different than what is displayed by TV today. What was Nightline's conclusion of the state of happiness in our country? Well, to give you a hint, the program began with the words: "If everything's great, why do so many people feel so bad?"

True, the gross domestic product (GDP) has been rising since 1973, but is the GDP truly an indicator of our happiness as a nation? The truth is that this figure can be somewhat misleading. In believing that this is a barometer of the happiness of our nation, one assumes that all purchases are made enhance our lives with happiness. The truth is however, that many purchase are simply made as a result of the demands of our society. For example, a woman that enters the work force will suddenly incur many expenses. She needs appropriate clothing for her job, a baby sitter for her children, possibly a maid for her house. Those things do not necessarily change her level of happiness, rather they merely allow her to maintain her position at work. A family may purchase a anti-theft devise for their car, an alarm for their house, install lights on the exterior of their home. But again, these do not show that their life is better, but rather that they feel there is greater cause for worry and suspicion.

The "liberation" of women and their entry into the work force was to have brought fulfillment for most, yet most women are less fulfilled now than ever before. Therapist, counselors, and Prozac are in great demand. Why? Because we are trying to go against God's design for women. God gave us the wonderful privilege of being the *heart* of our homes, our cities, our nation. This means that we have the opportunity to nourish and strengthen, even to set the very atmosphere of our surroundings, spreading encouragement, blessing and cheer. Yet our kind has rejected that role, wanting rather to be the head. We have rejected the structure of authority which God ordained in the beginning when he placed Adam under Himself, and Eve under Adam. God entrusted to Eve the care of Adam and their family. No small task indeed! Had she fought against Adam in her role and wanted to be her own boss and have her own way, it would have ruined the beauty and innocence of the Garden. In fact, it finally did! She disobeyed both God and her husband, and we continue to suffer the consequences today.

The Myth Called Feminism

Our precious role and high calling of being the *heart* is under attack. To really understand what is happening, perhaps we should investigate this goal of many in our culture called feminism. In the next few moments, we will look at its roots, its goals, and the course it is trying to take. It seems that it started in Eden, when Eve had been given everything that any woman could have wanted. A beautiful home, a lifetime shopping spree throughout the garden, a perfect husband (can you imagine being married to one who had never sinned!). But she rejected that, preferring rather "enlightenment" over what God desired for her. So she was indeed enlightened, enlightened to sin, to pain, to death. Yet just as she, those after her found great disappointment in life and have been forever seeking to fill the sense of loss that came as a result of the fall. Instead of seeking to please God in the earthly role He has given, we wanted a different role, we wanted man's. Yet in seeking to exalt women, feminism ends up doing exactly the opposite. For it is actually rooted in "misogyny," the *hatred* of women. Feminism is not simply the "advancement of women," it is seeking to nullify them. In making women "equal" with men, they really mean identical. And in wanting things to be equal, they are at once implying that to be a women shameful and weak, that it is we that must pull ourselves up to this "heightened position." Yet God wants us to glory in the beautiful and lofty position He has already given us, not to reach for something else, demeaning the very gift He has given.

And what are the goals of Feminism? Is is really just an innocent group of women suffering from poor self esteem? I think you will be surprised, perhaps horrified as you read the following quote from feminist Naomi Goldenberg:

"All feminists are making the world less and less like the one described in the Bible are are thus helping to lessen the influence of Christ and Yahweh on humanity... 'God is going to change' I thought. 'We women are going to bring and end to God. As we take positions in government, in medicine, in law, in business, in the arts and finally, in religion, we will be the end of Him. We will change the world so much that He won't fit in anymore.'"

Shocking, isn't it? Let's look at one more:

"The feminist movement in Western culture is engaged in the slow execution of Christ and Yahweh. Yet very few of the women and men now working for sexual equality within Christianity and Judaism realize the extent of their heresy."

A Matter of Design

Men and women are not interchangeable. If a pot made for cooking and a vase crafted for beautiful flowers decided to trade places, the vase would crack when placed over heat and the pot would do a poor job of enhancing the beauty of the flowers. In the same way, we can never expect to go against God's design and be fulfilled in doing so!

A Word to be Highly Esteemed

Submission is not a word for the weak. It is much easier for us to create our own agendas, make up our own minds, and be our own bosses. Yet strength of character is shown as one is able to submit her will to the will of the one she is serving. Jesus gave us the ultimate picture of submission when He subjected His will to the will of the Father that night in the garden. His own life hung in the balance, yet He was willing to give even that, that the Father's will might be accomplished in bringing our redemption. Surely the requirements for our submission dim in comparison to His.

True Success

America seems to offer a distorted picture of what success should look like for us as women. Our kind is seeking so hard to become "men" that the beauty and mystery of womanhood is being altogether lost. Many have bought the lie that the ideal position for a woman is climbing the business ladder, indifferent to those she may be stepping on as she moves up. An an aggressive, in-control woman is highly acclaimed in our world today. Many that are not "career women," have turned toward their money and leisure, trusting it to satisfy. Their fulfillment is sought in days at the spa each week getting hair and nails done, skin tanned, living solely for themselves. They may give money to certain causes, but even this is often done for others to see, or possibly make them feel justified in their self-indulgent lifestyle.

But long before feminism came God's ideal, which is hopefully yours and mine as well. This is the woman who seeks after God with her whole heart, with a meek and quiet spirit, who is humble before Him. Certainly, there is a great lack of support for this woman of godly beauty. We don't see it coming from Hollywood. No, this is not a set of traits that is seen by most as desirable. Yet, as we look across our country and the desperate attempt (of men and women alike) to find fulfillment, we see that they find they are empty, without answers. Countless rich, famous, "popular" people have finally shared that behind the pearly white smiles and fancy parties, their loneliness and emptiness consumes them. What a lie satan has spun! Who but our Maker can better understand His design for us and thus know where our true fulfillment lies? Does it not make sense to look to the God of the universe, the Creator of our very being, for His plan for us? As we look at Yaqar, we see that she was not out to "prove herself" to anyone, but rather to *give* herself away. And this with willing fervor! Elisabeth Elliot writes:

> *"We are called to be women. The fact that I am a women does not make me a different kind of Christian, but the fact that I am a Christian does make me a different kind of woman. For I have accepted God's idea of me, and my whole life is an offering back to Him of all that I am and all that He wants me to be."*

Rejoicing to be Women!

Are you glad to be a woman? Does that show to others around you? Does your dress reflect that you are grateful for the way God made you? This does not mean that lace and pale pink must dominate our wardrobes, but do we look like women, or does our appearance suggest we wish we were more like men? Do you know one of the primary reasons that I have been careful to keep a feminine wardrobe? Not as much for modesty's sake (although there are valid points to be made there as well), but mostly to contradict everything for which feminism stands. To emphasize the fact that there *are* differences between men and women, and furthermore, to express that I am grateful!

A Meek and Quiet Spirit

Are you gracious in your ways toward others? God has given each of us different personalities, no argument there. It is important to realize that, no matter what our personality, God tells all of us as women that we are to have "meek and quiet spirits." Some may have to work at this harder than others, but truly it is an uphill battle for all as it often flies in the face of the position our own will would rather take!

So what does it mean to have a meek and quiet spirit? Initially it may seem to describe a person who is shy, yet as we look at Yaqar's life, we don't read that she was a speechless women who kept her eyes riveted to the floor! It is so much more than the words that we speak, and the actions we display. It is the spirit *behind* those words and the intentions *behind* those actions. Most importantly, it is the peace that comes from knowing that God is truly in control of *all* things and is fully worthy of our trust.

Sometimes this means being willing to hold our tongue when we would rather get upset, to smile when we'd rather frown. This is not putting on a false front, rather it is digging deeper than our emotions in determining our disposition. There are days that we might feel frustrated by the actions of others, and no doubt there are times to exhort or even rebuke, but usually our initial response will be dictated by our emotions, not by the Spirit of God. Allow time for yourself to be calmed by the Lord and for your heart to be purified by Him in the matter before acting on your first response. Often our first responses will not lead us to live and react in meek and quiet ways, yet deep in our hearts we must remember that God knows our needs. We are not living for ourselves and our feelings, but rather to reflect Christ and the love that He showed for all of us. There is really only one character quality that Jesus attributed to Himself, and that was meekness. It is truly an honor that He would ask us to follow Him in this. It is interesting to think that our desperate world is trying to fit us with an "attitude," when God has already given us His beautifully chosen one!

"Secular Work"

Do you have a job that takes you daily into the secular world? If the Lord has laid it on your heart that this is His will for you right now, see it as a special position in which to proclaim the name of Christ. True, you may not be able to speak of Him as much as you would like, in fact, you may realize that doing so would cause you to be inattentive to your responsibilities and a poor testimony to those with whom you work. Still, ask God to give you other creative ways to testify of Him. Maybe you could design birthday cards with spiritual encouragement for those you work with, or ask God to give you special sensitivity to needs others might have. Or maybe He would allow you to use a generous amount of the money that you make from that position to support others who are in need. Someone once pointed out that the first job God gave to Adam was to name the animals. It does not sound like much of a "ministry" position, but obviously it was a task God wanted Him to do, one that was pleasing to Him. God intends for everything we do to be spiritual in nature, and we should always seek how we can commit each task to His glory.

We read in Acts of Lydia. There are really only three things we know about this honored woman. First of all, she was a worshipper of God; second, she had a special gift of hospitality; and third, she was a "seller of purple!" Certainly, she daily found herself in the marketplace, yet this likely gave her opportunities to witness that she would not have had otherwise! If we are working where others do not know Christ, even there may we seek to minster to those around while guarding against the "career" mindset.

Whether you work for someone that is a Christian or not, God intends that everything you do is unto Him and for this reason you should think of ever task as a ministry (both to Him and the others around). Do your job well, as unto the Lord, while at the same time, maintaining a servant's heart toward those around you. Without a doubt, mistakes will be made from time to time, yet humbly take responsibility and do what you can to fix these without bringing hardship on others around. See it as your goal to make those you are serving successful. Do not merely think of it as a job and a paycheck, ask God to help you catch a vision of how He might really make it a ministry and that your mind would be filled with this thought! One of the greatest complaints in management today is the near impossible challenge of finding capable, effective help. Determine to be a welcomed exception to this complaint! Have a willingness to go the extra mile as needed, and as you work enthusiastically "unto the Lord," you will find yourself refreshed in the process!

Give me an "E!"

The heart pumps blood to the body, giving life and nutrients to every member. As we have discussed being the *"heart,"* there are many exciting way that this can be lived out that we may not even consider. In teaching sign language classes, it has been fascinating to see the difference in each of the classes' "personalities." Right now, for example, I am teaching three separate beginner adult classes. Same material, same general ages of students, three drastically different classes. And one is excelling far beyond the others. Why is this? Well, although I am sure there could be many factors, one seems to dominate the others. In this most successful group is a woman who is always enthusiastic! Slightly tiresome at times, yet always enthusiastic! Although she is not a Christian and has clearly had a difficult life, she has certainly made a contribution to the spirit of the class. The others in this same class are inclined to share, to be actively involved, to participate with gusto, and outwardly demonstrate that they enjoy coming. Although my teaching style in all three classes is nearly identical, in the other classes, people are noticeably more quiet and inhibited. In this first class, they act as if they have known each other for years~ all spurred by the enthusiasm of one person!

If we have the spirit of God living within us, then we *should* have an enthusiastic attitude toward others! In fact, this word stems back to the Greek word "entheos," meaning literally "in God." Our enthusiasm comes not just from our personality, but from God living in our hearts! If we attend a class or church event, we should be sure that we do not sit with stone-cold expressions, but rather that our expression is one of encouragement to the one who is speaking. Even if this person is new to us, we should not make them "prove" themselves before we will show them a smile of acceptance. Learn to be a affirmer, nod if you agree, even if it be in a quiet way. We should show them that we accept them because of the love God has already placed in our heart.

We must be careful that in our enthusiasm, we do not become obnoxious! As we learn to show deference in our demeanor and become aware of what is appropriate in each situation, we will truly be able to be a blessing of enthusiasm to those around. Once a vitally important key to the balance of enthusiasm was mentioned in a seminar I attended. We are to be enthusiastic, yes! But we are to be enthusiastic in our *spirit*, not in our emotions. A person who is enthusiastic in her emotions wears people out and will likely be enthusiastic one day and discouraged the next. But one who is enthusiastic in spirit will encourage and contribute to others, and will be excited about learning and sharing in the lives of others. The enthusiasm will be deep in their spirit instead of on the surface in their emotions. This enthusiasm will be heard not in the loudness of the voice, but in the tone, not in the wildness of the action, but in the eager sincerity.

Enthusiastic in our Relationships

That enthusiasm should also carry over into our relationships with those around us! Convey interest in others, in their lives, in what they share with you. Although the Bible certainly exhorts against being busy bodies, there is a type of "nosiness" that I believe is actually important! One time as we moved GraceWorks to a new location, we had a small team of people helping to move our plethora of heavy boxes. One individual kept noticing things that no one else would see. Once, as we looked for a key, he said "I think there's one up on the piano behind a picture~with some writing on it." Wendy and I looked at each other and grinned, amused by his acute observation. Yet it was that same sense of interest that led him to ask some very thoughtful questions later in the day. As we shared about a difficult situation, he asked with concern "and was that ever resolved?" His question was appreciated because it showed that he both listened to what was said, and was genuinely interested in what we shared. It means so much to others when we show concern over issues close to their hearts!

Honestly, I would far rather someone be a little on the "nosy" side than to seem unconcerned and apathetic. If we share part of our heart with another and their response is nothing more than "Oh," we feel hurt, disappointed, like either they are not interested or do not care. As others share with you, do not be afraid to ask thoughtful questions. If they had not been willing to visit with you about a given subject, they would never have brought it up in the first place. There are certain instances that we should be careful about asking questions and caution that we are not contributing to gossip. To sense one's motive in asking questions is only to gather juicy morsels only harms the friendship. Can you be trusted by another that shares a burden of the heart with you? Trust is such a vital key! Once you have shown this genuine interest in another, make a mental note both to pray, and also that the next time that you meet this friend, that you remember to ask for an update! This kind of concern will mean more than you know.

In meeting others for the first time, we should seek to make them feel welcome. Even if our underlying nature is somewhat shy, God gives us the grace to greet people in a way that is warm and accepting. We can learn to ask questions and listen intently as they respond.

Taking Initiative!

Part of being enthusiastic is being eager to take initiative when there is a job needing to be done. If there is a table needing to be set, or a mess needing to be cleaned up, jump into the task and bring others with you! Some of the sweetest fellowship can be enjoyed when we are working together! Don't wait for someone else to take the lead, be a leader yourself. In the same way, if there is someone hurting, initiate a time of prayer. Offer "May I pray with you about this?" Not only are you bringing them immediately before the throne of grace, *they hear you* bringing them there. You may never realize how much this will minister to them.

While we are still talking about initiative, I should add that we must be careful not to squelch men's initiative. Often it is far too easy for us as women to "take over," when we need to allow men to learn to do so. If a man is attempting to assume leadership (whether it is leading people in prayer, in a project, or anything else), do all you can to support and encourage him in this, being cheerful but not overbearing. If there is a great need, and men present but no one initiating assistance, ask God to give you creativity. We often become impatient and "do it ourselves" instead of waiting for the Lord to put the pressure on them. Yet God designed men to be leaders and protectors. When we continually try to take over, we may find ourselves wondering after we are married "Why he never leads our family." We must be careful that we do not train men in the habit of allowing us to take initiative. This is a challenge at times, as our tendency toward sensitivity often causes us to see things that they may never realize. With a little creativity in such situations, we can encourage them to initiate by quietly asking questions like: "Is there anything we can to do help so-and-so?"

If we realize that God has everything in control and that the "king's heart is in the hand of the *LORD*," as it says in Proverbs 21:1, then we can be meek and quiet, knowing that since He is truly overseeing all things, we don't need to! Being meek and quiet, is not "doing nothing," but is actively putting our trust in *Him*. Glory in your womanhood~ it is a gift God has given! Purpose to stand against the world's concept of "equality" and stand up for God's *beautiful* plan for us as women! Shun being proud, having the "attitude," being domineering and easily upset by what may come your way. Ask God to help you speak in love, that you would be His *heart*, reacting even to difficult situations with poise and grace, as you deepen in your trust of Him.

*Q*uestions:

1) Have you ever expressed gratefulness to God for creating you as a woman?

2) Does your life show that you are grateful for this?

3) How is this demonstrated in the way that you live?

4) Does your life reflect a meek and quiet spirit, that you are fully resting in the Lord? What areas do you see that you are not resting in Him?

5) Would you say that you are an enthusiastic supporter of others?

6) What could you do to excel in this area?

*A*dditional Support:

• Verses: Gen. 1:27; I Cor. 11:3, 11-12; I Thes. 5:11; Col 3:23-24; Eph. 5:21; Rom. 15:1-6

• Resources: Singled Out For Him (Nancy Leigh DeMoss) A wonderful booklet subtitled "Embracing the gift, the blessings, and the challenges of singleness." If (Amy Carmichael) A very small book that though it could be quickly read in 15 minutes, its thoughts will cause you to ponder on even the smallest part~all day long.

She stretcheth out her hand to the poor, yea, she reacheth forth her hands to the needy.

I am only one,
but I AM ONE.
And I cannot do everything,
but I can do SOMETHING.
And what I can do, I WILL DO.
And what I will do, I MUST DO,
For I AM ONE.

I have never had a photographic memory, but when the above poem scrolled across the screen of a political candidates video, I vowed never to forget it. I reviewed it the rest of the day until I was certain it was etched in my mind forever. Maybe you will want to write it down and memorize it too. Such powerful truth it contains! For years I knew nothing of its origin, yet just recently I was surprised to learn that it was adapted from a poem written by none other than a woman that was both deaf and blind~ Helen Keller! She had limitations beyond what we could imagine, yet did not let them get in the way of what she could do. This overcoming spirit allowed her to have a deeper impact on this world than most ever hope to make (and perhaps we should note that had Anne Sullivan not poured her life into helping her, she never would have had been given such hope...).

His Hands, His Feet

God has put us on earth to know Him, and then through us He desires to accomplish His purposes. What an amazing thought! To realize that He would choose to use us, when He does not need us. And though at times we feel insignificant or as if our efforts could never make a difference, we must press, we must be faithful even in the "small things" God calls us to do.

A pastor told on a radio program about a little boy who would go out on the beach every morning and throw back out to sea all of the starfish that had washed up on shore. Another boy watched him doing this and mocked, saying *"What do you think you're doing? These are washed up every day, and there are so many, you can never save them all. You're wasting your time on something that will never make any difference.."* The boy was quiet a moment, and then responded *"But is does make a difference... it may not to all of them, but to the ones I throw back it does, to the ones I save it makes a difference."*

We can never evaluate our efforts by the broadness of the need, but rather by our obedience in ministering for Him, allowing Him to bring the fruit when and where He pleases. We can never know where our influence is the greatest, nor what broad impact our influence will have, even years later. A few years ago, another story was told which was so significant that, even though I can't remember the specific facts, I think it is worth repeating. The story was told of two men. One was brought under the influence of strong Christian teaching and training, the other was neglected and left more or less to fend for himself. The first man became a dynamic, caring minister, and the second a powerful man in the Mafia. These men, in just a few generations, had many born after them. Out of the descendants of our first man, more than one thousand became ministers or actively involved in the work of the Lord. Thousands were saved as the Lord worked through their efforts. And what of the other man? Of the men born after him, he too had more than a thousand born, and not surprisingly, they lived out their lives in the Mafia and in crime (which undoubtedly continues to this day). Can you imagine how many lives would have been changed had someone loved and reached out to one small boy so very long ago? But people were busy, and one little boy is not so important. Yet one little boy *is* important. And one little girl *is* important. For not only are their souls of great value, they may be the parents of generations to come, an influence for good or for evil.

Too Many Soiled Faces

Sometimes it is easy to feel discouraged in ministry simply because of the sheer vastness of the need. We live in a broken, shattered world, and to spend much time considering this is overwhelming. Yet God is not calling you and me to feed every hungry mouth, to wash every dirty face, to share the Gospel with every hurting soul. Someone once reminded me that even Jesus, when He was here on earth, did not heal every sick person and feed every one who hungered. He did *"the will of the Father."* It is easy for us to feel overwhelmed and give up completely, but this is not the answer!

Christian financial counselor Larry Burkett once received a letter about initiating a benevolence fund in the writer's church. Some of the members felt this was important, while others believed there were too many needs, making it impossible to decide which took precedence. His response was that we should never decide not to help because we cannot help everyone. He asked *"How many people could you help? Could you help five people? All right, then start by helping five people and if God wants you to do more than that, then He will make available the resources!"*

What about you? Who has God placed in your path for ministry? As one Bible study book challenged, do not just "start ministering," but look at where God is already at work. Where is He at work around you? Where are there hearts that seem to show a desire to know more of Him? What ground has He begun to soften? Although we can never fully understand what God plans to do in any situation, ask Him to show you where He is stirring hearts for His kingdom, and begin investing in these areas!

Exchanging Our Plan for His

Melissa was a young girl of thirteen that I met as I assisted an inner-city mission in a midwestern city. She came from a terribly troubled home and had already been smoking for a year when I first started working with her. In some ways she became almost like my own during that year, and I felt I could understand the agony of a parent who loves their child deeply yet watches as that child refuses to receive wise counsel and ends up in sorrowful struggles as a result. Although Melissa showed some progress during the time we were together, the environment of her home seemed to set her up for failure. Her mother lived in open adultery, and her older sister had her first baby at fourteen. Bugs and trash were everywhere.

I went back to visit a year ago, and when I walked in Melissa said not a word, but held me tightly for a very long time. It was apparent that our ministry to them had greatly touched their emotions, yet it seemed to have done little to change *them*. It was so hard to see her there, and I wished I could have somehow rescued her from the wickedness and despair of her world. She is 18 now, and has two precious babies of her own. Although I pray that someday Melissa will look back and realize her desperate need for the Lord, for His "higher ground" especially as she raises her girls, the present situation is certainly nothing for which I would have hoped and prayed.

During the year I was working there, two sisters were living across the street from her. These girls were very dear, despite their own rough upbringing and home situation. They brightened each time they saw us and really seemed to have a hunger for the Lord. We ministered to them in small ways, but our "focus" was on Melissa and her family. Recently, I have wondered if God brought us to Melissa's door so that we might meet and minister to her neighbors, who seemed so much more prepared and eager to learn of Him. Did our initial "plan" to minister distract us from what God had ultimately sent us there to do? It is hard to know for certain so many years later, yet it has caused me to be more alert as I evaluate and re-evaluate where and to whom God would have me minister.

Stepping Up to the Plate

Our responsibility to minister to the needy does not seem to be optional, just as Jesus says in the story of Matthew 25:34-46, *"For I... hungered, and ye gave me meat: I was thirsty, and ye gave me drink: I was a stranger, and ye took me in: Naked, and ye clothed me, I was sick, and ye visited me, I was in prison, and ye came unto me."* How easy it is for us to see needs around us, yet to be so caught up in our own plans and agendas that we fail to reach out. This was the problem with the three men in the parable of the Good Samaritan. They were seen by others as "holy" men, yet they did not show even the least concern for this one that needed their help so desperately. No matter how busy we are or what we are doing, the Bible says that we are serving the Lord Jesus Himself as we become involved in this realm. Additionally, as we feed the poor or meet the needs of the hurting~ not only are we helping others, but it is a strong reminder to ourselves of how blessed we are, and how much we have been given. So often when God gives us excess, we quickly use it on ourselves. But God gives us blessings, not that we hoard them for ourselves, but rather that we might have something to share with others. The early church seemed to understand this principle quite well! In Acts 4:32-35 we are told

> *"And the multitude of them that believed were of one heart and of one soul: neither said any of them that aught of the things which he possessed was his own; but they had all things common. And with great power gave the apostles witness of the resurrection of the Lord Jesus: and great grace was upon them all. Neither was there any among them that lacked: for as many as were possessors of lands or houses sold them, and brought the prices of the things that were sold, And laid them down at the apostles' feet: and distribution was made according to every man according as he had need."*

Think how exciting it would be if everyone who knew the Lord, gave to the poor as the early church did, and went a step further to help them learn to manage their households, and train those who were able with practical skills they could use in the workplace. Would welfare be necessary? Certainly, there are those who have a desperate need for outside support, and those of us who are able are compelled in Christ's love to help them. Many churches have funds specifically set aside to help those who are struggling in various ways. There is not always a simple solution to this problem. The Bible says *"if any would not work, neither should he eat." (II Thes. 3:10)* We must be careful that we do not enable one to continue in a behavior that is not only demeaning to them but which also takes advantage of others. There are times the most loving thing that we might do for someone is to withhold our gifts from them. At the same time, there are many that He will bring specifically our way that we might minister to them. Ask God to give you loving discernment as you seek to minister to others in this way.

Pocket Change

What about the quality of generosity in daily life? Are you a generous person, or do your actions reveal that *things* are more important than people? Although as Christians we have a responsibility to use our money wisely, we must never hoard it or think of it as our own. Having a generous spirit does not mean giving all one's money away, it just means that we do not hold on to it too tightly *("it is more blessed to give than to receive…Acts 20:35)*. How easy it is to damage a reputation in this area over what is simply pocket change! If someone is in need of a quarter, be eager to reach into your own change to find one. If you visit a new church, put something in the offering plate, even if you only have a dollar. This is in no way to show that you are a good person, but rather to demonstrate support and encouragement, a "vote of confidence" for your brothers and sisters in Christ. If you learn of a legitimate need, prayerfully consider if God would have you help in meeting it. If you are unable to do it yourself, maybe you could rally a team to become involved!

A Note of Caution

One final note-- we must be careful, that we are not pulled away from Christ by those we minister to, or even by close friendships that we have. We must be aware that in seeking to be a friend we do not lose our ability to be a positive friend to them~ or that in seeking to be a missionary, we ourselves do not become a missionfield. Satan would want nothing more than to pull you away from the Lord and will even try to use "harmless" things to do so. In both ministry and friendships, certainly there are some adjustments that we may make in deference to others. If we do not like fish, but one has prepared a trout dinner for us, we can graciously eat it. On the other hand, to participate in an activity or conversation that is not pleasing to the Lord, is not only a poor witness for Him, but we are more likely to become snared ourselves, than we are to convince others of their need for salvation. Often it becomes a temptation to begin to lower our standards, supposing that we might be better able to "win them to Christ." But more likely, even if they mock your high standard, deep down they respect you and you have become a beacon of hope to them. If we see that our desire for things of the Lord is dampened by the company of another, we must pay heed to this red flag of warning. For those of you that are younger, have a willing spirit toward your parents if they sense that a certain friend is not in your best interest. They are not saying this to be mean, but most likely because they dearly love you and would give their own lives for your well being. We could never imagine the love they have for us until we have children of our own.

I once had a friend I spent a lot of time with and whose company I enjoyed immensely. But I began to realize that as I spent time with her, I began to take on attitudes that were not pleasing to the Lord. I could not see how it would edify her for me to share this, but neither could I see how I could pull back from her without some kind of an explanation. I began to pray that the Lord would open a peaceful door of closure to our friendship. Very quickly He did just that. It was wonderful because I could continue to send her notes of encouragement, but the frequency of our times together changed nearly overnight and in a most simple way, the activeness of that friendship was brought to a natural end.

Adding Up!

It is true that you are only one. It is true that I am only one. But together we make two. And beyond that, there are certainly many others, making our number broad indeed! If we determine to be faithful to God's call (even in our small corner), then in a beautiful way, God will weave it all together to make a difference in this world! It simply starts by each of us asking ourselves "What would God have me to do today?" and then wholeheartedly taking that step in joyful obedience to Him!

*Q*uestions:

1) What do you think God would have you to do today? What about tomorrow?

2) What lives would He have you to touch?

3) Are you actively seeking to make a difference in the lives of those around you?

4) Write the initials of one you have sought to help in the last six months.

5) Is there someone to whom you feel God is calling you to minister that you are either avoiding or putting off? What hinders you? What do you believe that God is leading you to do? What is your plan?

6) Are there any friendships in your life you know may be harmful to you as a Christian? How might you graciously take a step back from these without thwarting future ministry toward them as individual?

*A*dditional Support:

• Verses: I Cor. 6:19, 20; Matt. 25:34,40; Acts 4:32-35
• Tools: Meaningful Ministry Pages~a way of keeping track of ministry to others.
• Resources: *The Lady of the Lamp; Florence Nightingale* (Basil Miller)

She is not afraid of the snow for her household...

for all her household are clothed with Scarlet.

I cried all the way home~ all four hours home. My parents had asked me to come home from college after my first year, and it was one of the most difficult events in all my life. I knew that God would have me to obey them, but I loved college and the friends that I had made there. How little I knew though, that through this obedience would come some of the greatest blessings of my life. I n the following months, I became increasingly excited and more fully convinced that the right decision had been made. Yet three years later, as I attended the graduation of my friends who had continued in school, satan began to bring great thoughts of discouragement to my mind. I began to feel as if I was somehow unsuccessful, that I had missed the opportunity to receive this valued document.

After the ceremony, the father of a friend walked over and said "Jennie, you know what I would like to see?" and then he pantomimed transferring the graduation cap from the head of one graduate, to my own. I smiled and thanked him for his concern for my welfare, but inside, it felt like a knife had pierced my heart. Deep down I knew that we had made the right decision, yet at that moment of weakness a struggle took place.

What is true success? Certainly God's definition is different from ours. He really does not care so much for "success," but rather for faithfulness. He wanted me to be faithful in coming home, in accordance with my parent's direction. For others, faithfulness would mean taking a different route, but for me, this was what God had asked.

Blessed Glimpses

I love people and have always had a passion for learning. I felt cut out for college, as it seemed such an ideal place for both friendships and learning. Yet God has allowed me to see so many of the rich blessing resulting from coming back home, that looking back now, I would be foolish to want it any other way. "Give up all of these years of incredible experiences and blessings~ for what once seemed so important to me? No way!" But other times God does not show us the purposes for our obedience so quickly. While visiting a Sunday School with a friend, I heard it wisely shared that trusting God, fully trusting in Him, means not demanding a logical explanation from Him for how He chooses to work in our lives. As Amy Carmichael remarked, *"(help me not) make much of anything appointed."* There will be things in our lives that seem overwhelming, which may never be understood this side of Heaven, yet beauty lies in their acceptance.

Although the Lord may ask us to live for years simply trusting in His promises of bringing "all things together for good," if I were honest, I would be among the first to admit, that when He chooses to give me a glimpse, I am thankful! It was only after a few weeks of being home from college that He opened so many doors of opportunity. Although it took more time for my heart to be aligned with His, He used these opportunities to encourage me as my will was being turned. One of my greatest interests was in the area of sign language, and I began to use it on a daily basis. I began a very interesting job in a law office, and involved in countless ministry opportunities that were of great excitement to me.

A Difficult Question

My excitement continued to grow, but then I would regularly hear a particular question from others "What about the future?" they would ask. "How will you support yourself?" the question often came. At first I was not sure what to say. I finally understood in *my* heart the vision that the Lord was giving, but how could I convey this to others?

Yet in time, some very logical, even exciting answers were realized! To begin with, I had no college debt to carry. To this day, nearly every one of my friends who graduated that day is still trying to pay off this huge sum. Most of them are married and have not only their own debt, but two. When I meet one of them for lunch, often this burden is a main topic of conversation. I am amazed at how significantly their lives, where they live and what they do, is controlled by the amount of money that they owe. One friend recently exclaimed that the desire to gain financial security for the future greatly motivated her toward getting a degree, yet the loans that come from that degree seem to be defeating that very purpose as she seeks to repay them now.

I think that a primary concern in the minds of individuals as they ask this question, is the trend of our nation that shows a very high ratio of men leaving their wives and children. If we are determined to marry not only men who claim to be Christians, but who love the Lord with their whole hearts and are living in determined obedience to Him, who believe that divorce is never an option, then we will likely never have to experience this. Of course, it is possible that the Lord could call them home early, but even in this, if God is not leading us to college, can we not safely trust in Him to "supply all our needs?" Furthermore, this concern assumes that one has no debt at her time of misfortune, yet what if this were to happen while a mountain of debt was yet unpaid? Not only would we need to work to support our family, but also to continue chipping away at this huge amount. And finally, a college degree rarely guarantees anything. Many men with impressive college degrees have struggled to find a job that could support their families.

His Leading

If you are going to college because you feel certain God is leading, and your parents are supportive, wonderful. I am not intending to imply that college is always a wrong choice. My purpose in including this is to help counter the mindset that there is no other way to be successful than to go to college. So many end up going simply because they don't know what else to do, or because it "just seems the thing to do," In the end, they often spend a lot of money and time for something they may never use.

God does not require a degree to do great work through us. Certainly we should never quit acquiring new skills and information. As I said before, I love learning! But there are often creative ways in which we can learn nearly the same skills, at much less expense. For some, college may be necessary, but be certain before you go. Eighty percent of those who get a college degree are not working in their chosen fields even ten years beyond graduation!

Not Walking Blindly

"Beware lest any man spoil you through philosophy and vain deceit,
after the tradition of men, after the rudiments of the world,
and not after Christ." Colossians 2:8

Toward the end of the book, we will talk about worldly philosophies that have made frightening inroads into our educational system. College is one such place where one can be exposed to a dangerous anti-Christian worldviews. I have seen so many excited, terrific young people go off to college and come back with faces of despair and a different set of values. If one is not very careful, the teaching received and the friends that are made can be detrimental to everything that one has grown up believing. I once helped a student with a creative writing project given my a Christian university. The question he was given read "When you are reincarnated, what animal would you like to come back as and why?" I could hardly believe the question~ not even *"if* you are reincarnated," but "when!" And this was a "Christian" institution! If any of you feel the Lord strongly leading you to college, even if it be Christian, I would highly recommend that you first go through Summit Ministries course "Understanding the Times." No matter how strong we may feel, we must be aware *"Let him that thinketh he standeth take heed lest he fall." (I Cor. 10:12)*

A Practical Example

I think that the following illustration will amaze you! Let's look into the lives of fictitious twin sisters, "Kari and Jodie." Although they are merely characters in our story, there is nothing that could prevent their story from being real, as it is based on actual facts. Let's say that Kari attends a college costing her $9,000/year, including room and board (a conservative estimate). We know that there will be many other expenses such as travel to and from school, clothing, etc. But just for her four years of basic college classes and board, she owes $36,000.

Now, on the other hand, let's say that Kari's sister "Jodie" decides to stay home and find a job that will teach her a marketable or beneficial skill and commits to saving as much as Kari is spending. Jodie still lives at home so her expenses are minimal and so even if she tithes, and gives to a worthy organization, helps with some of the bills at home, she still has plenty left over to take care of her personal needs. She has a job that pays $1,100/ month and puts away $750. Let's say that one year she even uses a years savings to purchase a car. Still at the end of those four years, Jodie has not only a car and the $27,000 she personally invested, she gained $2,830 in interest for a total of $29,830!

Six months after graduation Kari must begin to pay her debt, but since she has no experience, she starts at an entry-level position. Monthly payments (for a ten-year loan at 8% interest) are $437. The first year she can barely afford her payments. The second year, she is better able to pay, yet she needs a car, among other things and continues to struggle paying the minimum. She gets married to a man who has a similar debt, and now, as a couple, they have two to pay, totalling over $60,000. A few years later they make the financially difficult decision for Kari to stay home with the children. This will mean an incredibly strict budget, yet they feel they have no other choice. By the end of fifteen years, Kari's debt of $36,000 (at 9% interest) has cost her more than $50,000. Between her and her husband, they have spent over $22,000 in interest alone. They have no savings, or significant personal assets.

Jodie gets married as well. They choose to set her savings account aside to save for the future, and will never add a dime to it beyond what Jodie put away during her four years of savings. Not only has their marriage has not had to bear the incredible strains of debt that Kari and her family have experienced, but by the time these debts are paid off, Jodie's account has reached $54,000~ over $24,280 in interest alone. *The real key comes now with the secret of "compounded interest."* Though they could use this money at some point to purchase a home, if they place a it in a money market account (at just 6% interest) for 40 years, their total will be more than a quarter of a million dollars~ a staggering $323,000! And this grew out of nothing more than the money Jodie put away during those four years!

Additional Options

All right! You may be feeling convinced by now at the ways the Lord can work even without a college degree (and considering how you are going to spend your $323,000!), yet possibly you are asking the question "What are other options?" As I came home from college, I was encouraged to investigate opportunities in which I could "apprentice." This simply means learning a trade or ability by working under another in an area of skill. I shared before about working in a law office. It was a wonderful experience as I worked, not only with many Christian lawyers (yes, there are a few!) but I also had an opportunity to see first-hand much of what is involved in fighting for justice. I made nearly daily trips to the courthouse and learned more than I imagined in the process! I later worked in an inner city health clinic and my eyes were opened to the needs of people right around me. I worked with precious deaf children in the school system who patiently helped me as I learned more of their language. I was able to go on mission trips to Russia, to New Zealand. I traveled throughout the midwest with a ministry groups as we focused on encouraging young people and families. Best of all, I came to know and love my family in a way that I never had before. As I think about it, there were more exciting twists and turns than I could ever record or even remember!

For those of you in this situation, seek ways of gaining skills in areas of your interests, ask the Lord if He might not only provide someone who is proficient in their field but one that is a godly individual as well. This will double your learning. And then you complete the circle as you seek to bless them. Whether this starts as a paid position, or if you are working as a volunteer, or in exchange for the training being given~ be diligent in your work, and eager in your learning, communicating enthusiasm in your work. Take advantage of every opportunity to learn, and as you do, seek to bless others!

When people would ask Michael LeFebvre, a brother in the Lord I met in ministry years ago, what he was doing with his future, he would share the verse in I Corinthians which says: *"Eye hath not seen, nor ear heard, neither have entered into the heart of man the things which God hath prepared for them that love Him."* Then he would humbly share "If I could imagine it, it would likely be far less than what God has in mind!~ if I concentrate on being faithful to loving God as this verse exhorts, I can also trust that God will be faithful to lead in what He has prepared..." In considering the story of those who *"did this (ministered to tangible needs) unto the least of these,"* and in effect did it unto the Lord Jesus Himself, Michael realized that an outlet of loving God, was expressing this to others in seeking to meet their needs. He felt that for him to attempt to fully plan out his future would lessen what God really had for him. And I think he is right~ how can we ever imagine what God has in store, even for the next year! If we seek to love God and serve others, we will never be at a loss for things to do!

More than We Could Imagine

Although there is nothing wrong with having great aspirations for the future, if our focus become stayed on our own ideas or plans, we may become distracted from what God's deeper plan for us might be! I cannot count the "simple" jobs I have found myself doing, that later gave me the background to make important decisions or to embrace future opportunities with greater skill or accuracy. Had I known the whole path earlier, I may have become disgruntled with the present as I awaited the future. Little would I have realized that this was God's way of equipping me with the tools I would need, and of Him to building His character in my life.

Never underestimate God's work or the importance of faithfulness even in the "small things" of today. None of us know what is in the works for tomorrow! I must also say that, just as I am humbled to see how the Lord desired to minister through the skills He led me to learn, it also disappoints me to think of all of the "small" ways in which I have not been faithful to His call. What more did He want to do that was blocked by my own willfulness, lack of patience, or wanting to do things "my own way?"

The Bible tells us that there is only one debt that we are to owe, and that is the debt of love. Furthermore, Jesus said "If you *love* me, feed my sheep." Yet God often uses the skills that He builds into our lives, and our knowledge and understanding of Him, as the tangible ways in which He nourishes others. And as we invest in these areas now, only God knows the dividends that they will pay~ both now... and for eternity!

Due Respect

While we are discussing debts, may I slip in a little request here for all of us to consider? Often we speak of "paying respect," as if it were a debt to be paid, and in that light, there are three areas I would like to mention, where paying such a debt is often not considered.

One of the Ten Commandments instructs us never to use the Lord's Name in vain. Do you know that when ancient scribes would copy the Bible word by word, they would use a new quill each time they wrote the Name of God? In fact, they revered His Name as being so holy that they refused to even speak it! Yet today it is often used as slang or in other ways that are in no way respectful of Him. Some have found other words that "substitute" His Name that may seem to "soften the effect" a little, yet still falls far short of that unspeakable awe we should pay His holy Name. To even use a substitute for it in a moment of surprise or frustration, causes us to become casual about what is holy and encourages others to do the same.

If we as Christians are not careful in the use of it, should it be a surprise that others are unaware of the respect that is due Him? To think about it practically, there is no need, purpose, or benefit in doing this, unless we are indeed crying out to Him. Not only does it show Him disrespect, it does absolutely nothing to change or better our situation! May we learn to use all of our words carefully, but especially when referring to the God of the Universe and His Son who spilled His precious blood for our redemption!

Secondly, can you imagine what those who lived their whole lives waiting for a Bible, or who were imprisoned for their possession of this Holy Book, might think to see a Bible "plopped" on the floor, or treated in a disrespectful manner? We often do these things without thinking, yet to realize, we have the precious, holy Word of God... I have been challenged by people that have decided, simply out of respect, not to place their Bible on the floor. After considering it, I have tried to adopt this principle myself~ and I do not see it as a rule, but rather as a privilege. If I have no other option, sometimes it is at least possible to place something else beneath it. Certainly it does not harm my Bible to touch the floor, just as it does not harm the flag of our country for it to brush the ground. Yet in recent years our forefathers would burn such a flag~ not because the flag had changed, but because they did not want their respect for it to dim, or for their hearts to become casual about that for which so many had given their lives. In the same way, it will do our own hearts and minds good as we show outward respect for His Word~ the message for which He gave His life.

One other area that is worth considering is the way that we dress to go to church. Non-Christians or new Christians may come to church dressed as they are ready to go to a ball game, and we should receive them with open arms and not even take notice of their attire. But for those of us that have known the Lord, we should find joy in showing respect for Him in this way. Although God is always with us, going to church is a special time each week we set aside to specifically and directly honor Him. We would never stand before an earthly king in careless clothing if we desired to show Him honor.

Although two of these three areas are not specifically commanded in Scripture, I would encourage you to consider them before the Lord, simply as ways you might choose to honor Him. Again, I see these as a privilege and can imagine times that they might need to defer to a greater command. If, for example, an elderly person suddenly needed assistance, I would not hesitate to put my Bible on the floor in order to help them. These are simply ways that I like to honor God in my own heart and to possibly somehow communicate that sense of respect to others. At the same time, if I became self-righteous in this decision, satan would be winning the victory and it would matter little where I placed my Bible. The heart is the key.

It seems the bottom line to areas such as these, is that as we become more casual about the Lord in the way that we talk and act, we may unconsciously be chipping away the last remaining respect that our country has for an Almighty God. In a court of law, those in the courtroom hear the instruction "all rise" as the judge enters. This does not change the *judge's* position, but it reminds the *individuals in the court* of the honor of this position and supports his authority. In the same way our actions can have an effect on the way that those around us view the God that they observe us to worship!

"May the words of my mouth, and the meditation of my heart,
be acceptable in Thy sight, oh LORD, my strength and my Redeemer."
Psalm 19:14

When God first saves us, we come to Him broken and in desperate need of not only His salvation, but also His sanctification. After we are saved He begins working on our hearts and changing us from the inside out. As He works this change in our hearts, we are truly able to then "give of our best to the Master..."

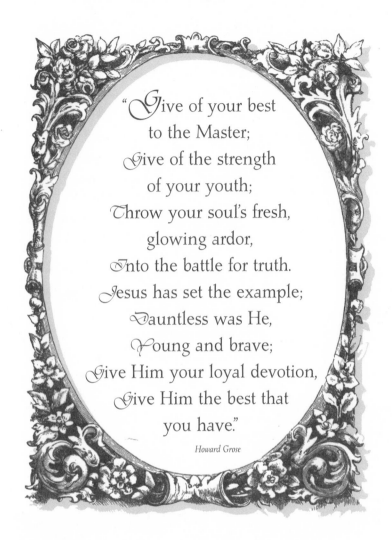

"Give of your best
to the Master;
Give of the strength
of your youth;
Throw your soul's fresh,
glowing ardor,
Into the battle for truth.
Jesus has set the example;
Dauntless was He,
Young and brave;
Give Him your loyal devotion,
Give Him the best that
you have."

Howard Grose

Questions:

1) Have you established a savings account? Don't wait until you have "extra" to start or it will never happen! Although in time you will reap the benefits of compounded interest, you will also be prepared if an unexpected need would arise!

2) Do you work from even a simple budget? It is a wonderful way to be able to see how you are using your money, as well as great preparation for the future!

3) In what ways do you sense God is leading your life right now?

4) How do you think your outward actions toward things of the Lord affect others?

5) How can those around you tell that you love and respect the Lord if they were only to see the outward evidences in your life?

6) When you consider giving of your best to the Master, what do you think that this means in your own life?

7) Is there an area discussed in this chapter in which you realize you need to consider? If so, what is it?

*A*dditional Support:

- Verses: Proverbs 10:7; Romans 13:8; Isaiah 64:4; I Corinthians 2:9

- Resources: Crown Ministries Classes, I was greatly blessed by taking one of these years ago. A wonderful course which teaches exciting Biblical principles of money management.

She makes herself coverings of tapestry; her clothing is Silk and Purple

*T*wo people enter the room, on your right enters one with a pleasant expression, shoulders back, her hair in place. Her clothing is attractive and pressed, the items she carries, cared for and ordered. The one on your left shuffles in wearing "tired-looking" clothing and a somber expression. She has unkempt hair, a mess of books and papers in her arms.

Which of these would you choose to run a vital errand, to deliver an important message, to pick up your precious little sister or brother from across town? While outward appearances can often be misleading, there are times when a person's character comes shining through. True, the second one to enter could have a sweet and tender heart, but we don't know that, and have no time to find out. All that we can see is that she is quite disheveled and if she struggles to keep herself together, it seems risky to trust her to come through for us. It also may tell us that she doesn't respect her person as a temple of God, or possibly that she is lazy, or a number of other things. What does your outward appearance tell people about you?

1/21, A Small Fraction...

I have struggled greatly in considering the inclusion of this chapter as it wanes in importance to every other chapter in this book. The Bible specifically exhorts us as women to focus on inner beauty of the heart. Yet the fact is that how we look on the outside is seen as a representative of what is on the inside. Anne Ortland, author of many books including "Disciplines of a Godly Woman," pointed out that only one of the twenty-one verses of Proverbs 31 relates to appearance. She then stated that our appearance should take just 1/21 of our time and effort, whereas the gaining of skills and character the other 20 parts. This seems to be a wonderful equation. Appearance is not a major part, yet it still has its place in the fraction. If I expect my car to function, I cannot neglect to put the key in the ignition and turn it. It is a small action, especially when compared to the efforts given to build the car, maintain it, and the concentration given to operating it. Yet it is part of a bigger picture. In the same way, while keeping this area in its rightful position, it seems to demand a degree of attention.

His Radiant Child

How does a woman look who loves the Lord? What should be her distinguishing external qualities? Though there could likely be great differences in opinion about how one should look, I think there are some basic, yet very important principles upon which we would all agree. First of all, as His jewels, our greatest focus should be on having a countenance which reflects the One that we love, and nothing that would distract. Such a beautiful verse is found in Isaiah 61 describing the Lord's adorning of us.

> "I will greatly rejoice in the Lord, my soul shall be joyful in my God; for He hath clothed me with the garments of salvation, He hath covered me with the robe of righteousness, as a bridegroom decketh himself with ornaments, and as a bride adorneth herself with her jewels."

A wedding ring is typically characterized by a diamond, which reflections the love of a man for a woman, and his commitment to her.

In the same way, our dedicated and love for others can be a symbol and reflection of the love and commitment of God to mankind.

The diamond however, cannot abide by itself, and is attached to a golden band which supports it, holding it in place. The gold is not the focus of the ring, yet the band will either enhance or distract from the diamond. If the gold is gaudy, it can take away from the luster and beauty of the jewel, and by the same token, if the gold is tarnished and dull, it does little to enhance the diamond.

Squeaky Clean

Just as God's beginning point for us as Christians is to purify our hearts, so the basis for our "temple" is cleanliness. I have been reading in Leviticus lately, and it is amazing to read of the cleanliness that the Lord required of the Israelites, both spiritually and physically. The rashes that are described as unclean would have certainly sent all of us "outside the camp" more than once! Yet God knew, thousands of years before we knew of the existence of those little things we call germs, that they could be very destructive to His beloved nation Israel. He put requirements upon them that other nations did not have, but this was for their own benefit and survival.

God has redeemed our hearts, and He desires that we testify of His redemption to others. I have met some of the dearest people who have the most diligent hearts for the Lord, who outwardly would turn many people away because of their carelessness in areas of hygiene.

Make sure that you smell clean and fresh. If you are one who has chosen to use "natural deodorant," be certain that it really works! There is a difficult situation here as I can understand the reasons one might have for stepping away from the more traditional mode. The problem is, that this may work for some, but not for all. A person can become accustomed to body odor and become quite unaware of it. You might want to ask a trusted friend if they have noticed this unintentional offense! It might also be wise to have some "real" deodorant on hand to use occasionally for events that might make you especially nervous (and more liable to sweat!). I'm certain natural deodorant works for some, it's just more apparent when it does not!

That Healthy Glow

Some of you have worn make up since you were 12 or 13, others have chosen not to wear make-up at all. Of course, I cannot say whether one should or should not wear make-up. I do, but some of you may have a personal conviction against wearing it. If that is the conviction God has given to you, then you are right to continue in that. A clean bright face can radiate His love beautifully.

One friend of mine does not want to wear much makeup, yet has perceived her own need for a small amount. In seeking to minimize this as a focus in her life, she has chosen to only wear foundation and mascara. Though we each may see God leading us differently in this area, it is vital for us to remember that no matter what we decide, our faces must most importantly shine forth the love and patience of Christ. In any case, it is far more important that we "prepare our faces" spiritually, than that we prepare them physically.

Again, especially in this chapter, I am not trying to create an outward ideal, but rather share what has helped me and allow you to decide before the Lord what He would have for you. My purpose in writing this chapter was to encourage us to each seek the Lord in this area, and help us to consider, if we have not already, the responsibility we have as an outward reflection of the Lord.

I can't recall exactly when I started wearing make-up, but I remember a friend's mother sat us down one day to teach us about skin care and the basics of this new routine. I remember it being fun and sort of embarrassing, all at the same time. I don't remember much about those years of attempting to perfect this art, but it is amazing how much there is to learn and how many mistakes there are to be made! Trying to look natural, yet refined, bright, yet not shockingly so. Yet being raised in a family where makeup was simply a part of getting dressed in the morning, we have often teased my mother, that "don't forget your lipstick!" will be forever etched in our minds!

If you read the book of Esther, they certainly did a lot to enhance her beauty, and God used that to His glory (and truly, some of us may need this extra help more than others!). Yet her focus was not on her appearance, but on the Lord as she entreated the Lord with three days of fasting and prayer, that she might please the king and gain a hearing with him that her people Israel might be spared.

A Good Beginning

When you choose makeup, be sure that it looks natural with your skin type. My sister and I cannot easily share makeup because our coloring is so different. At one point my skin was prone to breakouts and I can sympathize that it is much more difficult to keep makeup looking natural when this is the case. Possibly the most important key to well-done makeup is clean skin~ be faithful in washing your face at night, even if you are half asleep! Taking Vitamin E is very good for the skin and will be good for many other body systems as well!

Perhaps the most important thing that I could say about makeup is that it can be a great time-stealer if we allow have much attention. In fact, when I consider any of the "daily" activities of my day, I will often look at them in the light of a year. If I daily need fifteen minutes for any one activity, then I must realize that it is taking more than a hundred hours a year. In other words, if I spend fifteen minutes each day on my makeup, I am spending well over four days (and nights) applying makeup! (Yuck!) I have whittled my makeup routine down to five to seven minutes, slightly longer for a more formal event. In fact, I have pushed my entire morning routine, shower included, down to 30-33 minutes! Again, I have to use my timer to motivate myself to work this quickly, but even that is a joy as shortening this task has somehow simplified it in my mind! Even if I am weary, I am much more inclined to dive on into this routine knowing it really does not take me very long to complete.

Hair

Hair may well be more important than makeup. Clean, sweet smelling hair that is under control allows one to look well-kept. I am aware that a few of you reading this wear head-coverings. You have done well in that you can very easily achieve all of the principles I am going to present here quite effectively!

The Bible describes our hair is our glory. *(I Cor. 2:15)* Although I would be challenged to show my face in public without at least a little makeup, I believe that well-kept hair is of greater importance. If our hair is messy, our whole appearance looks messy, and the makeup can seem almost like a facade. Your hair should frame your face, and draw attention to your smile, not cover or outdo it! If you feel uncomfortable fixing your hair, ask someone you respect for advice!

Dress

Often it seems that the highest priority for dress today is personal comfort, and we forget to consider any other factors. Have you ever thought about ways in which your dress could benefit others and yourself as well? Studies have shown that people are treated quite differently, simply because of the way they are dressed. The way you dress (or don't dress) tells others a lot about you. If you are wrinkled, musty, or too casual for the occasion, people may think that you are lazy, indifferent, or possibly that you lack understanding and training in what is appropriate. If we are living for the Lord, and have a message of His to share, we cannot afford to let down in this area.

A few years ago I spent a lot of time traveling. I wish I had counted the number of times that I sat in an airport next to an older woman who actually thanked me for the way I dressed (and I did not feel I was terribly "dressed up" I would usually wear just a simple dress~ something comfortable, yet clean and pressed). So many would comment about the ultra-casual dress of many young people today. Most of these women were quite frank about how they felt toward this trend and expressed great disappointment in the way that most dressed, whether they be traveling, shopping, or out to eat.

Our aim is not to be "dressy," or to outdo the dress of everyone else. There is no purpose in wearing a starched suit to a picnic, but it is important to consider what message we are putting forth by the clothes that we wear. When you are dressing for an occasion, consider what is most appropriate. You are not seeking to stand out because of your dress, but rather to dress to match the message your life has to share.

Shining like Stars

If I were going for a job interview at a local bank, I certainly would not dress shabbily, with messy hair and go without a bath. No, I would press my clothes, shower and fix my hair so that the one interviewing me could see that I knew how to take care of myself, and therefore could likely take care of others. If I wore torn, dirty clothes that did not fit, how could I be expected to take care of the property of others? In a much greater way, we must consider that we are dressing for the service of the Lord!

One of the most difficult lessons we have learned in GraceWorks is the importance of the outward appearance of our products. We initially worked so hard (for years!) to be sure the product was of excellent quality. Yet we found this was not enough, we could not make ends meet. The product had to be *packaged* in a way that was attractive. This made our cost go up, but it made a difference in sales as well! Why? Because though we are told that we should not "judge a book by its cover," we *nearly always do!* If we like what we see, we investigate further, if we do not, then we go on to something else. The Bible says in I Samuel 16:7 *"for man looketh on the outward appearance, but the LORD looketh upon the heart."* We have often quoted that verse and focused only on the second half, inferring that the outside does not matter very much. And certainly it does not matter *as* much, but it does matter! It says *"man looks on the outside."* Our priority is indeed what God sees, yet as we are seeking to make a difference in the world, we must not neglect to consider the initial message we give.

Possibly I should not hesitate to point out that the way we dress may also be adjusted at times in order to further our ministry. Of course, this cannot be used as a reason that we should dress sensual in our day, for this would violate God's Word. Yet there are times that we may need to alter our outward appearance to some degree in deference and seeking to selflessly love others. Hudson Taylor is a wonderful example of one that saw he could better minister to the people of China by taking on their native dress, and the people loved him for his heart to identify with them in this way. At one time my sister ministered within a community that did not wear makeup and she made adjustments as to not be offensive to them. Different situations may require different responses however. One missionary tried to take the dress of the people, and to her surprise, they did not approve! As we are sensitive to the Lord, we can trust that He will give us wisdom in using deference in necessary situations.

Chocolate Prunes

If I were to buy a box of chocolates, and got home only to find it full of pitted prunes, I'd be dreadfully disappointed! In the same way, if I was looking for a diamond ring, I would begin my search where things sparkled, not in the oatmeal aisle at the grocery. If we dress just to "keep up with" the fashions of this world, and if on our faces we maintain the same somber or snobbish expressions (or "attitude") as those of this world (smiling at only those whom we claim as friends), how will they ever know that we have something different? That we have hope in Christ? If our "packaging" advertises us falsely, how will they know where they might find godly answers and encouragement, or see what God can do with a life that is submitted to Him?

From the sheep to the silkworm...

I am broken-hearted to see how the enemy has even whispered into many church youth groups and girls come clad in shockingly sensual or sloppy ways. We often eagerly grab up whatever is the newest rage, and throw common sense out the window. I believe it is often unintentional, but nevertheless we have a responsibility to honor God in this area just as much as any other. So often it seems that little thought is given to what is or is not pleasing to the Lord. When our dress is sensual or sloppy, it is certainly a challenge to strongly uphold a bright, holy testimony of a life which has been transformed by the glorious power of the Lord.

I could talk until I was blue in the face about modesty, that it is a gift we owe to our brothers in Christ. Yet possibly it would be better coming from a couple of them. First of all, let me allow you to step in on a conversation I had with a friend from church, as he pulled me aside during a retreat years ago. "I don't quite know how to say this..." he stammered, "but I just want to thank you for the way that you dress. A lot of us guys were talking, and we all agreed that one of our greatest times of struggle in keeping our thoughts pure is at summer retreats. Girls just don't understand... I just wanted to thank you." His words surprised me... and at the same time they did not. We often forget (and at times ignore) the need we have to respect our brothers in this way. How I appreciated the honesty of my brother in Christ, for it caused me to be more firm in my attempt to be a pure vessel through whom the Lord could work. A great part of our problem is that as girls, as women, we are made up so differently than the men folk. To us we see an outfit and think it is "cute," but what we must realize is that if we have not been discerning, to a guy the same outfit may be sensual and cause him to stumble.

A speaker recently shared that "in the past it took an entire sheep to clothe a woman, but now a silkworm can do it on his lunch hour." This puts it in a slightly humorous light, yet often it seems nearly the case. It shows so little respect to our brothers when we let them down in this area. There is enough for them to fight against~ from magazines in the check-out line, to billboards that attempt to catch their eyes. Don't be yet another stumbling block to them!

Many of you may be familiar with Josh Harris, author of "I Kissed Dating Goodbye." He issues a similar challenge to all of us as he addresses this very area. He says *"many girls... would look great in shorter skirts or tighter blouses, and they know it. But they choose to dress modestly. They take the responsibility of guarding their brothers' eyes. To these women and others like them, I'm grateful."*

May we accept the challenge issued by these men, and unspoken by many others, and may the purity of Christ sink so deep in our hearts that it would permeate this and every other area of our lives.

Hints... at no extra charge!

1 I have appreciated the advice to mostly buy clothing that is "classic" in style. I remember when bright fluorescent colors were in.

Those who filled their closets with these had to replace them the next year when they were "out" or choose to wear clothes that were recognizably "outdated." When I was a teen-ager, "jelly shoes" were the rage (some of you remember~ soft plastic shoes in every color under the sun~ a few pairs even made their way into my own closet!). Thankfully these were a fairly cheap trend, but as with other styles, they quickly came and went. At the same time, I have clothes that I purchased ten years ago and am still wearing today because their classic lines transcended time better than their faddish counterparts.

2 Make it your goal to look nice and well groomed, but do not aim to be up on this month's style and trend. Not only is it financially detrimental to over-haul your wardrobe so often, if you dress, look and act like everyone else on the outside, others may logically assume that you think the same on the inside. To focus great amounts of time and attention on your clothes may communicate that they are more important to you than they really are. I am not suggesting that we should have no sensitivity to style. Paying little or no attention to our clothes and appearing frumpy will not profit the goal of radiating Christ either. In fact, it could even cause people to reject our message~ if outwardly we are falling apart, how can they believe we are any different on the inside?

3 Be aware that one dress may be very nice on a friend, but may not flatter your shape at all. The color can also be an important factor. Although I have never had my "colors done," I think there is reason to consider what colors look best on us. You may love pastels, but against your skin they may not add any radiance at all. Maybe ask a friend or your mom for advice on what colors look best with your coloring and skin tones.

4 What are some of my favorite places to shop? Would you believe Goodwill or the Salvation Army? If you have never been to one of these stores, it may be an adjustment, but you are in for a real treat! We probably cannot buy our whole wardrobe there, but it certainly helps stretch our budget. I recently purchased a brand new dress for $2.97, and get complements on it every time I wear it! By the same token, beware! It is easy to buy clothes at these places because they are "such a good deal" and wind up with a closet full of clothes that we don't want to wear! Only buy clothing that you *really* like, and when you bring a new item of clothing home, retire an old one!

5 Don't get caught up in name brands. Name brands often simply mean giving more money to a company that likely has more than enough anyway, for a product that would be worth much less were their name not on it! Not only might it be an unwise use of God's money, it might also cause others to feel greater pressure to do the same. At times I *will* look for a certain name because I know that its quality can be trusted to last and is thus a better investment.

6 Dress to draw attention to your countenance, not your body. Do we really want to do anything that would cause one with a reprobate mind to think lustful thoughts about us, let alone, as we said before, to cause a dear brother to stumble?! True, men will be held accountable for what they think, but can we really assume that we will not also be held accountable if we make ourselves a stumbling block?

Posture & Manners

Once we are dressed and ready to be a "sweet fragrance," we can ruin our look by poor posture. Many have noted that we should imagine we have a string tied to the top of our heads, pulling us upward, and should allow our bodies to fall in line with that string. Keep your shoulders back in a comfortable position, hold your head up, and smile! Sit up straight when seated, but remain comfortable. You are seeking to show that you are interested in listening and in what is going on around you, not that you over-starched your shirt! Balance is the key!

My eyes were drawn to a beautiful woman as she entered a restaurant. She was well put together, her hair seemed flawless. She intrigued me as she sat down and gave her order to the waiter. Yet as her dinner was placed before her, she became a monster! She leaned way over, never looking up, inhaled her food, getting it all over herself in the process! I could hardly finish my own meal with this scene taking place so close to our table! Then, as quickly as it had begun, it was over. She wiped her mouth, and although she looked the same as she had when she walked in, to me she appeared quite different.

Manners, not just when we are eating, but in daily life is a final piece to the puzzle. If we are put together at first glance, but quickly fall apart soon thereafter, then it is all for naught. And it seems that manners are rooted in one simple phrase from I Corinthians 13, "If I... have not love, I am nothing." Love for others above ourselves is the root of every beautiful manner we will ever learn.

Questions:

1) When you dress, do you consider how you should dress for the message your life is seeking to communicate?

2) How would you sum up that message?

3) Are there any items of clothing that you realize you may need to get rid of in deference to your brothers in Christ?

4) Consider your posture. Does it show outward interest in others (vs. apathy) and an eagerness about life?

5) What would you say most greatly threatens your ability to "shine like a star?"

Additional Support:
• Verses: Rom. 12:1,2; I Cor. 6:19,20; Phil. 2:4; II Cor. 6:3; Eph. 5:1,2; 8; Matt. 5:14-16

Her husband is known in the Gates, when He sitteth among the Elders of the Land.

Truly, our husband *is* known in the gates! Thankfully in America, our Heavenly Father and Husband is still loved and worshiped, even if many are trying to dethrone Him. I was amazed, and immensely grateful, that as our currency was redesigned, "In God We Trust" remained unchanged. In the midst of so much hate toward God, what a blessing to see such reminders of Who has made our nation great.

In considering the sad state of our country, I think back to the Tower of Babel. To imagine trying to reach the heavens by a building project seems pretty silly now as we better understand the atmosphere and our true relationship to the "heavens" they were trying to reach. They thought they were making good progress, yet we can only begin to imagine how far they really had to go! I wonder how "silly" we must look to God when we act as if our efforts could dissolve His power or existence. We take down nativity sets, pull prayer out of schools~ yet does this change God or lessen His power? No, of course not. But certainly it must disappoint Him to watch those He created, the people He died for, treating Him with such contempt.

It says in Scripture *"He that sitteth in the heavens shall laugh, the Lord shall have them in derision"* (Psa. 2:4). To think that we could believe, even for a moment, that we could do anything to send even a slight tremor through the throne of God is unthinkable. We could just as easily move Mt. Rushmore by blowing on it. Frank Peretti once shared in a message, of the movie *"Out on a Limb"* by Shirley MacLaine. He explained that as the movie climaxed, Ms. MacLaine is seen out on a beach, waves crashing, shouting at the top of her lungs with arms outstretched, *"I AM GOD! I AM GOD,"* the audience is stunned, filled with a surge of self-empowerment and strength. Yet in the midst of this most powerful scene, he imagines for us a scene taking place in heaven~ the Angel Gabriel says to the Angel Michael *"Hey, take a look at this"* And as the angels peer down from heaven, Mr. Peretti repeats Ms. MacLaine's boisterous claim, only this time in a sheer, tiny falsetto voice *"I am god. I am god."* It makes us laugh to imagine his illustration, yet such fitting commentary! How important we can make ourselves feel through "self actualization" and "raising our self esteem" yet in truth we are still just simple, sin-filled humans, in desperate need of a Savior.

A Once Great Nation, changing...

Our nation was founded upon godly principles. But godly principles go directly against our willful nature as humans. We want to do whatever we can, whenever we want, to make up our own rules, and then to be excused from suffering the consequences of our bad behavior. Yet for those who have refused to submit their will to His, their only recourse is to make this attempt to eliminate God from society, exchanging Truth for the religion of Humanism. We see this being done on many different fronts, the least of which is education.

On reason that education is so susceptible, is because when we see something in black and white type, and here it from many "respectable" sources, we quite readily accept it as fact. As we read earlier, Hitler knew that if he could control the education (thus the way that people believed) the control of the nation would soon be his. So how is this bing done in our educational system today?

Read this as taken from an article in *"The Humanist"* magazine:

> *"The battle for humankind's future must be waged and won in the public school classroom by teachers who correctly perceive their role as the prose-lytizers of a new faith...*
>
> *"The classroom must and will become an arena of conflict between the old and the new—the rotting corpse of Christianity...and the new faith of Humanism."*   *"A Religion for a New Age," The Humanist, Jan/Feb 83*

And the following statement given at a 1973 educational seminar:

> *"every child in America entering school at the age of five is mentally ill, because he comes to school with certain allegiances toward our founding fathers, toward our elected officials, toward his parents, toward a belief in a supernatural Being, toward the sovereignty of this nation as a separate entity.*
>
> *"It's up to you teachers to make all of these sick children well by creating the international children of the future."*

Evolution, Man's Attempt to Create Himself

One way many educators are trying destroy our godly foundation and promote Humanism is through the teaching of evolution. Although there was never a time in my life I believed evolution to be true, I never considered it a direct enemy of Christianity ~ rather as an errant belief of those that did not believe in creation. But I have appreciated the ministry of Ken Ham, as he has brought this issue to light in the minds of many. As he has wisely asserted, if people believe that they evolved from nothing, then there is no God to whom they are accountable. If there is no accountability, then it is truly up to man to create laws for himself. If he can justify abortion, fine. If he can justify homosexuality, no problem either. He is his own creature, why shouldn't he decide what is right? And those that say "This is wrong, this must stop" are simply being intolerant, seeking to "force" their own personal view on the lives of others.

But on the other hand, if they had not been so strongly convinced that evolution was true, possibly there would be more of a concern in their heart "what if I am wrong?" For them to be wrong would mean eternal consequences, ones they would shudder to consider. It is much more comfortable for them to continue in error, and live the way "they have a right to live." And yes, maybe they have a right to live that way, but it is grievous to think of where it will take them someday, if their hearts are not changed in time. May God use us to begin to plant "seeds of doubt" in their hearts! (more in book two!)

How solid is the theory of evolution? I have often heard it said that it takes more faith to believe in evolution than it does to believe in creation. Why then, is there such an adoration of this theory, and why is it being taught as if it is fact? Very simply for the reasons shared above. Our world does not want to consider that there is a God to whom they are responsible. How determined are they to hold onto their beliefs? One well known scientist went so far as to claim that even if *every proof* pointed *without doubt* to the creation account of origins, he still would never accept it. The simple truth is that their tightly-held worldview *needs* for evolution to be true. And so it stands.

A colleague of Darwin spoke out at once against his theory, saying that his teachings had given every criminal justification in his misdeeds. He furthermore cautioned that if his writings were believed, that humanity *"would suffer a damage that might brutalize it and sink the human race into a lower grade of degradation than any into which it has fallen since its written records tell us of its history."* Does this not describe condition of our world, the immorality of our nation, the killings taking place within our own cities and schools?

What did Darwin think of his own theory? In "Origin of Species," he shared in chapter six *"Long before having arrived at this part of my work, a crowd of difficulties will have occurred to the reader. Some of them are so grave that to this day I can never reflect on them without being staggered..."* He later wrote of the discrepancies he found, saying they were *"all undoubtedly of the gravest nature..."*

In "Darwin's Leap of Faith" we read that these difficulties weighed heavily on him for many years, and that he was *"well aware that scarcely a single point is discussed in this volume on which facts cannot be adduced, often apparently leading to conclusions directly opposite to those at which I have arrived."* Indeed, Darwin was "deeply conscious of his ignorance." In his personal letters he wrote of having *"awful misgivings"* of having *"deluded myself"* and of having *"devoted myself to a phantasy (sic)."*

One Nation, Under God

A second primary way this war of elimination is being fought is through altering of our pages of history. George Washington stated in his farewell address: *"Do not let anyone claim to be an American, if they ever attempt to remove religion from politics."* Yet this is exactly what many are doing. I recently purchased two resources that covered different parts of world and US history. Though each were from different sources, I was shocked by the obvious changes and omissions within. When one looks at the early documents and writings of our founding fathers, quite a different story is told than many textbooks would lead us to believe today. Our nation was founded by godly men that loved the Scriptures, and God's hand of blessing has been on our country for many years as a result. Yet Humanists know that if people believe this, it will only damage their anti-God agendas, and they are trying hard to see that it is suppressed. The frightful truth is, that the further we as a country move from God, the less of His protection and blessing we will experience.

But what is the truth about the founding of our nation? What did our founding fathers really believe? Though you will not read it in history books, thousands of unaltered pages of history make this position impossible to defend. What did history really say of these men? Here are just a few examples, pulled from hundreds which show what they believed, and how they thought our nation should be governed.

John Adams, our second president said:

> *"We have no government armed with power capable of contending with human passions unbridled by morality and religion. Avarice, ambition,*

revenge, or gallantry would break the strongest cords of our Constitution as a whole goes through a net. Our Constitution was made only for a moral and religious people. It is wholly inadequate to the government of any other."

Patrick Henry stated:

"It cannot be emphasized too strongly or too often that this great nation was founded not by religionists, but by Christians, not on religions, but on the Gospel of Jesus Christ."

Consider this resolution passed by the U.S. Senate on March 3, 1863:

Resolved, That devoutly recognizing the supreme authority and just government of Almighty God in all the affairs of men and nations, and sincerely believing that no people, however great in numbers and resources... can prosper without His favor, and at the same time deploring the national offenses which have provoked His righteous judgement, yet encouraged in this day of trouble by the assurance of His Word... through Jesus Christ, the Senate of the United States do hereby request the President... by his proclamation... to set apart a day for national prayer and humiliation."

Entertain Me!

It is no secret that most movies today are presenting ideas that are contrary to God's ways. Yet it is common to think that it is the "way our world behaves," rather than seeing it as a direct attack against the God of the Bible, seeking to propagate negative thoughts against His ways and conditioning us to accept what we know to be destructive, sinful patterns.

"The church as all powerful, has been replaced by films." George Lucas

In a recent issue of the Christian news magazine "World," there was an article called "Hollywood Heroism." It said that *the Soviet Communists knew what American conservatives are just now learning, that the way to take over a country is not through politics but through shaping the culture."*

"the Soviets made a concerted effort to infiltrate and control America's entertainment industry, from taking over the trade unions to influencing the writers, actors, and directors who were creating the American imagination... As documents newly released from post-com-

munist Russia confirm, the Soviet spymasters and espionage agents
were directly engaged in America's arts and entertainment scene."

Lloyd Billingsley
"How Communism Seduced the American Film Industry

Wow! Is that as shocking to you as it was to me? And so often we
tend to believe that what we watch is merely entertainment, and fail
to realize the dangerous "education" we are simultaneously receiving.
Not only must we be careful in what we watch because of the ungod-
liness to which we are in danger of being exposed *("And have no fellow-*
ship with the unfruitful works of darkness" Eph. 5:2), we also must beware that
we not allow our resistance to be weakened to carefully packaged
lies~ the theories and philosophies quietly being promoted. Often we
begin by "putting up" with something, only in time to see ourselves
beginning to accept it. May we never come to the place of tolerating
evil. We must love the sinner, but if we embrace the evil, then we are
no longer a vessel God can use to share with them the freedom and
eternal deliverance that only Jesus Christ can offer!

"Sin is a Monster of such Awful Mien,
That to be Hated Needs but to be Seen.

But Seen Too Oft, Familiar with Face,
We First Endure, then Pity,
then Embrace"

Alexander Pope

I am sitting in a hotel in Knoxville, TN, grateful for a few days God
has given at the end of a conference to work without distraction. As
I sat here typing, I suddenly heard the noises of a marching band. "A
parade!" I thought. I looked out my window and though I could not
read any of their signs but watched the marching band as it walked
by. The trees kept me from seeing very much of the parade at once,
but I took a picture of it to mark the memory. It was such a colorful
parade with multicolored balloons and marchers. *"How wonderful to have*
a parade march right by one's window!" I thought.

But my heart sank as I saw a band of rainbow being carried by the
marchers, and suddenly realized the ugly reason behind the colorful

balloons. It was a "gay pride" march, complete with disrespect to God and His design for mankind. I felt sickened and it was difficult for me to return my thoughts to writing. I marvel that they have chosen to use this beautiful symbol that God gave to Noah. Of course, it is good to remember that it is *God's creation,* and only taken by them. God still owns the rainbow. As I sat back down to write I had to ask God's forgiveness for our nation and for my own apathy toward sin. *(Ironically, at two in the morning I heard another sound outside that same window. Although it was not an intrinsically beautiful sound, it was "music to my ears." I ran to the window, and would you believe, a monstrous street cleaner! I was refreshed to watch him as he sent pressurized soapy water across the ground they had earlier traversed. God was giving an incredible picture~ how He must want to sweep his cleansing power across the hearts of our great land...)*

Although legislation will never change the hearts of our nation, we need God's blessing shining down upon us and must do all that we can to see that our laws are pleasing to Him. Furthermore, in creating a moral climate, a natural result is that people will seek the Author of those morals. If people believe there is no right and wrong, then there is no realization of our need for forgiveness when we err. After watching these colorful but lost people walk by, I somehow felt dirty myself and wondered of the sorrow God must feel to see such a sight. Knowing I had not previously taken any pictures I could not live without, I finally opened my camera to expose the film, wanting to rid my camera of this image. It was an interesting analogy to me, to think that as the light flowed in, it washed away the very record sin, for the picture could not abide when the light shone in.

Responding to Those Who Live in Darkness

We know it must begin with us. How often in recent years we have been reminded of the challenge in II Chronicles. 7:14; *"if My people, who are called by My name, will humble themselves and pray, then I will hear their prayers and heal their land."* How desperately our land needs healing. In fact, fearfully so. Read the words of Thomas Jefferson, which are etched in the famous Jefferson Monument in Washington, D.C.

> "God who gave us life, gave us liberty.
> Can the liberty of a nation be secure where we have removed a conviction that these liberties are a gift of God? Indeed I tremble for my country when I reflect that God is just.
> That His justice cannot sleep forever..."

We must realize that there is a serious battle that is being fought over the souls of men. At times it seems that the enemy is winning. Again and again that quote rolls over and over in my mind, *"Evil triumphs when good men do nothing."* What are we doing to stand up for truth and morality in our country? Though it is not an easy road, it is one we must walk with courage. Do whatever you can to stand for righteousness in your city. Has a seductive picture been raised up on a billboard for all to see? If this is has been done by an otherwise respectable company who is seeking to use sensuality to promote themselves, write a note sharing your great disappointment as well as the reason for your concern. Send a similar letter to the company owning the billboard. Be careful that you are not hateful, but that your tone is factual and concerned. If the billboard is "adult" in nature, write to your mayor or city leaders and share with them your concern. If there is a law about to be passed that is contrary to God's laws, write a letter to share your concern with those who are in power.

Our family is sad that our state is often associated with a group of people who have chosen to react in a most awful way to those involved in the homosexual lifestyle. Armed with crass posters and mouths full of horrible comments, they picket homosexual events, including their funerals, (which must be one last blow for heart-broken parents to see). I wonder how this must grieve the Lord Jesus who truly loved sinners as He confronted them in their sin. I appreciated hearing a (previously homosexual) man tell the story of his conversion. He ran a store where a Christian couple would often shop. One time he became very sick. He did not know that any of his customers would even notice, but what a surprise when this Christian couple showed up at his door one night, with groceries and a hot supper. They ministered to him during that time of illness, and then one day the husband came in and sat down with his Bible. He then very quietly and lovingly showed this man God's plan for men and women. This man was stunned by the love that these two showed to him, and in time turned his heart over to Christ, turning his back on the lifestyle that once ruled his life. The love and fragrance of Christ had truly changed his heart.

Whenever we witness to another, we must remember that satan is trying to destroy them, that sin destroys sinner. Once the exterior is pulled away, they are just one lost, hurting soul that desperately needs the salvation of the Lord.

> *"The things that will destroy America are*
> *prosperity at any price, peace at any price,*
> *safety first instead of duty first, the love of soft living,*
> *and the get rich theory of life."*
>
> Theodore Roosevelt

Recent polls have given great cause for encouragement. For the first year since 1967, college freshman changed the liberal trend by expressing more conservative views than their elder classmates. It seems that as our society begins to reap the consequences of a faulty, man-centered belief system, there is renewed willingness to reevaluate what one has believed to be truth.

If you have a computer, create a personal letterhead and keep important political and local addresses stored where they are close at hand. Once you have your first letter formatted, those written thereafter will often take only moments to complete!

We must also be certain to write letters of appreciation when billboards are changed or good laws are passed. Often it is easy for us to complain but we forget to respond positively to good when we see it! If you see a store making choices that are moral (such as choosing not to sell certain items), let them know of your support!

When writing a letter regarding a law or bill to be passed, simply specify the number of the bill (ex: HR-6), whether you support or oppose, and why. It is really that simple. Of course you can add other information such as statistics supporting your view, or your own background that might strengthen your position as a knowledgeable writer.

Remember as you write, the perspective of your recipient. If we say "God's Word says *(X)* is an abomination," yet they do not believe in God or the Bible, then we might as well be telling them we found it in the writings of Kermit the Frog. If they have no fear of God, telling them what God thinks will have no meaning whatsoever to them. This point just scratches the surface of what David Barton shares in his wonderful video on presenting truth to a secular audience. I recommend it for all of you, not only for consideration in political issues, but also because it gives food for thought in seeking to share the Gospel. We first must help one to begin doubting what they already believe before they will be open to what we really have to share.

In her book *"I'd Speak Out on the Issues if I Only Knew What to Say,"* Jane Chastain encourages "letter-writing parties." Whether it be a distasteful billboard or a dangerous law being passed, invite friends over for an afternoon or evening dedicated to this cause. Be sure to use different styles of stationary, some hand written, some typed. She suggests you might even give prizes for the most creative, the most persuasive and so on. Write a different day of the week on the area that the stamp will be placed, and have each person take their letter home so that they will be mailed at different times from different places. You might also have one person write a letter to the editor of your local paper. It can be a most enjoyable evening~ others can bring snacks or you can provide a refreshment for them. You could easily make it a once a month event and go to one another's homes! The most exciting part of all is that those in government count each letter they receive as representing 100 people (assuming that others feel the same way but have not written). If you have even five people writing, that is equivalent in the minds of legislators, to 500 people!

Most important of all, at the end of the evening, pray that the hearts of the receivers will be open to what you share. Pray that their hearts would be turned not just in the issue at hand, but toward the Lord for eternity. One prayer that I have often prayed for those in authority or influence *"Lord, turn their hearts toward You and Your ways and may their influence on this world be in direct proportion to their love for You."*

Stand Up, Be Counted

One of the most important things that we can do as citizens is to vote. Men have given their lives that we might have this right, and thus we have the opportunity to elect wise candidates who will make prudent decisions. Although it is true that the nation is not going to be turned back to Christ through politics, politics still has an important role in our ability to honor God as a nation, and in our freedom to worship Him. If the judges and politicians who write laws for our nation write moral laws, then they support the truth that there is a moral law, thus laying the foundation in the hearts of citizens that there is absolute truth. And absolute truth lays the foundation for belief in One who laid down that truth. Do what you can to encourage others to vote. You might offer to baby-sit for a mother as she votes or pick up an elderly person who could not get there herself. The Christian community has a enormous number of votes, and the potential of turning any election~ if only we would exercise this right!

Our Greatest Need as a Nation

Above all, we need to be praying for our country, praying for our leaders, and asking for God's mercy on behalf of those that will not ask for themselves. There has never been a time in our nation when we have ever been more desperate for God's healing and revival to spread across our land. Could you be depended upon as a prayer warrior for your country? Could those that have yet to trust in Him, someday thank you for your prayers on their behalf? Are you interceding, "standing in the gap" for anyone today?

"And I sought for a man among them, that should...
stand in the gap before Me for the land,
that I should not destroy it:
but I found none."

Ezekiel 22:30

May the Lord never have cause to "find none" with us. May we be
faithful to stand~ even if we feel we are standing alone.

To Whom it May Concern~ Sample letter:

S a n d y   S h e t l e r
1001 Brown Oaks Drive, Springhill, PA 15144

June 14, 2010

The Honorable Tom Smith
House of Representatives
Washington, DC 20515

Dear Congressman Smith,

*I am very concerned about the effect the bill, HR-461 could have on our
country, and would ask that you vote against it. I have personally witnessed
the damaging effects of gambling in our community and believe that the passage of this bill would only lead to greater destruction.*

*Having worked with families on welfare, I am aware that they are espe-
cially vulnerable to losing their money in hopes of "one big win." In reality, it
only places thousands of families in more difficult circumstances than before.*

Thank you for your consideration in this matter.

Sincerely yours,

Sandy Shetler
Sandy Shetler

Be certain to pay extra special attention to grammar and spelling!

"But the Lord said to me,
Do not say, "I am a youth,"
because everywhere I send you, you shall go,
and all that I command you, you shall speak.
Do not be afraid of them,
for I am with you..."
Jeremiah 1:7,8

"Therefore, thus says the Lord,
If you return, then I will restore you– Before Me you will stand;
And if you extract the precious from the worthless,
You will become My spokesman.
They for their part may turn to you, but as for you,
you must not turn to them." Jeremiah 15:19

*Q*uestions:

1) For those of you with computer access, design a personal letterhead. It needn't be fancy, just ready for use!

2) Who is one person in your community or in the nation that you will write a letter to this week? This could be a letter of concern, or simply a note of encouragement! Return here when you finish to affirm your task is complete!

3) Do you "stand in the gap" for others? What about for your country?

4) Who would God have you to be "standing in the gap" for right now?

*A*dditional Support:
- Verses: I Kgs 18:21, 37-39; II Chron. 6:36-40; Ez. 22:30; II Tim. 3:1-5
- Resources: Darwin's Leap of Faith (John Ankerberg & John Weldon), *Faith of Our Founding* Fathers (Tim LaHaye)

Chapter Eighteen
Accepting the Challenge!

Well my friend, I believe congratulations are in order as you have courageously reached the end of this volume! Yet I hope you do not truly see it as the "end" for an exciting road lies before you now! Eagerly consider what God would have you do from here in order to make a difference in your world! Some of you may see that you must begin by asking God to begin to change your attitudes, and to start allowing the Lord to work more of Himself and His love for others within your heart. Others of you have willing hearts, but possibly lack action and need to work on setting an actual plan in motion. Most of you have likely experienced a mixture of success and failure in both of these areas, and may be blessed by working through many different aspects held within the chapters in this book.

Review your purpose statement once again. What further thoughts have come to your mind as you have read this book? Are their any changes you would like to make in it? As I conclude, may I leave you with a challenge? With your purpose statement in mind, bow your head and commit these next twenty-eight days of your life to the Lord in a special way.

Spend a few minutes mapping out these next four weeks. Turn back to the table of contents and indicate the four chapters you feel are most imperative for you to focus upon right now. Write these in your notebook and you will have before you you initial "plan" for the next month! Choose one of these to begin brightly tomorrow morning! As you get up tomorrow, re-read this chosen chapter, the questions, and your answers to them. Look up Scriptures that pertain to that area (you may want to find more of your own!), and begin meditating on them, asking the Lord to renew your heart after Him in this area. Next, write out how you will purpose to strengthen this area this very week. Every day, every morning during your quiet time, work on memorizing the verses and "setting your mind" on God's will for you in this area. Once you get to the end of the week, seek to record all you have learned and how the Lord has worked in your heart and life. Then you will be ready to tackle a new chapter! Certainly, there will still be improvements to be made in this first area, don't be discouraged as you have taken great strides in the right direction~ and you can easily reflect upon a chapter and your notebook at any time!

We can be overwhelmed in attempting to change everything at once. But the exciting thing is the direction you are heading and where it will take you! Ask God "what is my growing edge? Where should I begin?" In a marriage seminar the question was asked "What could you do today that would improve your marriage just 10%?" This is a wonderful question we can ask ourselves in modifying it to "What could I do today that would improve my life, my relationship with God and others just 10%?" This breaks a bigger picture down into exciting little "bits" that we can eagerly tackle one by one! As you consider this, what additional activities need to be included to move you toward the goals God has given to you? What activities need to be excluded? (remember to focus not only on your practical goals, but the goals of the heart as well!) Making a difference is not just a one time effort, but a whole lot of daily things, that ultimately add up to a life that is prepared to make an impact on others.

As you close now, asking God to make these next weeks driven by His purposes and for His glory. Ask Him to give you the grace and strength to live for Him in a way you may never have before. The first days may be difficult, and if they are not, then difficult days will come. There is an enemy fighting against you as you go. Yet *"greater is He that is in you, than he that is in the world."* If you feel discouraged, remember, you're not acting on feeling, but on what is right. Most often, as Frank Bettger has said, emotions will *follow* the action! Don't live tomorrow while it is still today, as that grace won't arrive till midnight or after!

What this comes down to, is whatever you want to be doing in the future, you must begin doing now. You must not wait for tomorrow or satan will hand you another excuse on a beautiful silver platter. As the Bible says to our lost world; "today is the day of salvation" so today is the day of renewed purpose and life for you, for God may well be wanting to work through your life to make a difference in theirs, to draw the world to their Savior.

Pastor Mishki was imprisoned in a Communist prison for 22 years, not even knowing of the welfare of his wife and six little children. A Communist was in the prison cell with him. One day, the Communist asked Pastor Mishki "Tell me in one sentence, what is Jesus like?" The pastor thought for a moment and replied, "You wish to know what Jesus is like? He is like me." The Communist said, "Then I will love Him and respect Him."

Initially we may be shocked to read that a mere man would compare himself with Christ. Yet are we not to be like Christ as Christians? Are we not to seek to become like Him in every area of our lives? What else does it mean to be "Christ-like?" Yet if someone asked you to explain Christ to them, could you say "He is like me?" How far are we from being able to say this ourselves! How can we do to fully "put on Christ" in every area of our lives? What does it mean to deny ourselves and follow after Him?

I am praying for each of you as you finish this book, and would be glad to know that you are praying for me as well. The road is rough, but God is good. As you are able to complete the given challenge for the next twenty-eight days, I would be glad to hear from you and know what God is doing in your heart and life! God's blessings to you as you seek to serve Him ~ as *His chosen bride!*

Lovingly,

"Now unto Him who is able to keep you from falling and to present you faultless before the throne of grace, to Him be honor and glory forever and ever, Amen!"

For information about
items mentioned herein,
contact us at:

Grace Works Ministries

1421 Lieunette
Wichita, KS 67203
(316) 269-3013

Areas
of
Volume Two

• *Making Life Beautiful*

• *The Two Secrets of Contentment*

• *Getting Beyond Heartache*

• *Becoming a Faithful Servant*

• *Becoming a Gracious Person*

• *Being a True Encourager of Others*

• *How to Skillfully Counsel Others*

• *Being a Rich Blessing to Your Own Family*

• *Effectively Discipling Others in the Lord*

• *A Foolproof Way to Memorize Scripture*

• *Restoring Your Own Heart by Forgiving Another*

• *Waiting... With No Knight on the Horizon!*

• *An Exciting Plan for Dynamic Leadership*

• *And...*

(more!)

Bibliography:

Though every attempt was made to give credit to each individual quoted, in cases where the information was lacking, we will continue searching, that proper updates might be made in future editions.

Chapter Three

1. Elisabeth Elliot, *A Chance to Die; the Life and Legacy of Amy Carmichael*, (Old Tappan, NJ: Fleming H. Revell, 1987), 31

2. Basil Miller, *Florence Nightingale* (Minneapolis: Bethany House Publishers, 1975), p. 125

3. Richard Taylor, *The Disciplined Life*, (Minneapolis: Bethany House Pub., B. H. Press, 1962), 23

4. Moody Adams, The Titanic's Last Hero, (W. Columbia, SC, The Olive Press, 1997), 19.

5. Ibid., 25

Chapter Four

1. Joshua Harris, *I Kissed Dating Goodbye*, (Sisters, OR, Multnomah Press, 1997), 21

2. Stephen Olford, Social Relationships (within a message given at Moody Bible Institute)

Chapter Five

1. Basil Miller, *Florence Nightingale* (Minneapolis: Bethany House Publishers, 1975), 25

Chapter Six

1. Paul Marshall, Their Blood Cries Out (Dallas, Word Pub., 1997), 14

Chapter Seven

1. Richard Taylor, *The Disciplined Life*, (Minneapolis: Bethany House Pub., B. H. Press, 1962), 22

2. Ibid., p. 24

Chapter Nine

1. Richard Taylor, *The Disciplined Life*, (Minneapolis: Bethany House Pub., B. H. Press, 1962),,33

2. Amy Carmichael, *If*, (Fort Washington, PA, Christian Literature Crusade, 1996, ~from 1938 original publication), p55

3. Richard Taylor, *The Disciplined Life*, (Minneapolis: Bethany House Pub., B. H. Press, 1962), 37

4. Jonathan Edwards–Philip E. Howard, Jr., *The Life and Diary of David Brainerd*, (Grand Rapids, Baker Book House, 1949), 24, Resolution 63

Chapter Eleven

1. F.R. Beattie, *Apologetics*, (Richmond Presbyterian Committee of Pub., 1903), 37,38

2. Clark Pinnock, *Set Forth Your Case*, (Nutley, Craig Press, 1967), 7

3. N.A. Woychuk, *You Need to Memorize Scripture*, (St. Louis, SMF Press, 1993), 92

4. George Mueller, *Answers to Prayer* (Chicago: Moody Press)

Chapter Twelve

1. Joshua Harris, *I Kissed Dating Goodbye*, (Sisters, OR, Multnomah Press, 1997), 91

Chapter Thirteen

1. Naomi Goldenberg, *Changing of the Gods: Feminism and the End of Traditional Religions* (Boston, Beacon Press, 1973), 4

2. Ibid., 10,3

3. Elisabeth Elliot, *Let Me Be A Woman* (Wheaton, IL, Living Books, 1976)

Chapter Sixteen

1. Joshua Harris, *I Kissed Dating Goodbye*, (Sisters, OR, Multnomah Press, 1997), 99

Chapter Seventeen

1. Charles Darwin, J.W. Burrow (ed.), *The Origin of Species* (Baltimore, Penguin Books, 1974), 205

2. Ibid., p. 315

3.Ibid., p. 66

4. Francis Darwin (ed.), *Charles Darwin; Life and Letter,* Vol 2, pp 232,229

5. *Congressional Globe,* third session of the Thirty-Seventh Congress, pp. 1448,1501

6. Gene Edward Veith, *"Hollywood Heroism"* World Magazine (Ashville, NC, God's World Publications, March 20, 99), 19

7. Lloyd Billingsley, *Hollywood Party: How Communism Seduced the American Film Industry in the 1930's and 1940's.*

Could we with ink, the ocean fill,
and were the skies, of parchment made,
were ever stalk on earth a quill,
and every man, a scribe by trade.

To write the Love, of God above,
would drain the ocean dry,
nor could the scroll, contain the whole
though stretched from sky to sky.

Oh, Love of God!

How rich and pure,
How measureless and Strong!
It shall forever more endure,
The saints and angels song!

F.M. Lehman